A WHITE MASTERPIECE and
Other Novellas

CAROL PHAM

A White Masterpiece and Other Novellas
A Kindle Direct Publishing

Softcover ISBN: 9798394799570

Hardcover ISBN: 9798393266776

Manufactured in the United States of America

DEDICATION

This book is dedicated to my loving Mother.

It is unrequited. This filial love is unreturnable and I will never be able to repay for every sacrifice she has made.

Love and appreciation to all you have done. I love you, everything, Mom.

-A White Masterpiece

"You give but little when you give of your possessions. It is when you give of yourself that you truly give.

I am only one, but I am one.
I cannot do everything, but still I can do something.
I will not refuse to do the something I can do."

-Catherine Musco

A WHITE MASTERPIECE and OTHER NOVELLAS

A rose is a rose is a rose…-Goodwin.

ACKNOWLEDGMENTS

I acknowledge Grandpa Phu for his help in writing this novel. There are many things that Grandpa Phu says that would lighten up the whole page. I even think he wrote the whole thing. He taught us guilt and there is no one with more compunction than my Grandpa. Maybe he cares most about us. I am sure there will be more of us after Judgement day on Earth and Heaven alike, where there will be immortality.

We should be fully equipped until then. Let's laugh then for he is quipping in with us and one day we shall be there.

Expedition one. Listen and you will hear in August Rush the sounds.

Life is not an illusion and don't let what you see fool you.

Take time and don't toil with haste. There is more to life than money.

Love is patient, love is kind. Love is not jealousy...

Dear Family...

You will enter the realm of heaven if you know nothing. She is an angel.

We are adages. There is the youngest but not... Always a fancy saying.

Remember, somehow matters are arranged as such and we are only the players in a board game of checkers. Someone is doing the thinking for us and everything has been allocated.

Thank you for your participation in this life and I hope we enlist again the next time. That is it for now and let the journey begin in readership.

READERSHIP

Elegance of Writing

Eloquence of Speaking

The Power of Read

Reading is learning. Most likely whenever you read you learn something new. If you love to read then you will love to learn and in return you will reap smartness and intelligence. You will have context.

If reading is our passion then we will learn the library. Many people who love to learn read plenty.

Positive feedback of *The Power of Read*

Power is knowledge. Knowledge is learning. Learning is reading. Reading ability is power.

Power is the ability to read. Reading is learning. Learning is knowledge. Knowledge is power.

It can go on. Power is winning...in love or in war?

Myth: People know reading is always positive no matter what, but there are always distractions. Because of everyday life activities, people are too lazy to read. Are people smart because they do not find time to read and have other preferences? No, they read when they find time. There are distractions and lack of concentration but what can be more fun and exciting than reading if we organize it and know its advantages. It is just picking up a book and starting to learn.

People love to read but what are the advantages compared to the similar intelligence faculties/*powers* of writing and speaking. Follow the positive feedback to comprehend the power of reading. Only reading can gain you knowledge.

Reading is diligent/*hard* *work* and rigorous/*meticulous*.

For those who love to learn, simply read. You don't have to search in the wilderness. The eyes are the window to the soul...a picture is worth it a thousand words. Many things are worth seeing to comprehend its meaning infinitely. You can imagine dragons...find out can rainmakers be bona fide/*true*? Words and intelligence can turn your imagination into the endless beautiful wonders of the ancient world and today's innovation.

What is your favorite genre? Fiction or nonfiction. Fantasy or science fiction. I hate romance, that's why I am how I am. The Disquisition at Pencil Point. Essay Walden. On Civil Disobedience. I like it to be in touch with nature and tranquility. The Vatican Prophecy. Know the origin of the Roman Catholic Church where the Pope resides. Conclave and election of Popes by Cardinals worldly event. Read from renowned influencing writers of ancient time such as James Joyce, Mark Twain, Joyce Carol Oates, Scotts Fitzgerald, William Gaddis, Emily Dickenson, Herman Melville and Jorge Luis Borges to indispensable subsequent generations of influential writers like Theodore Dreiser, J.K Rowling, Robert Fulghum, Ken Follet, Simon Winchester and A.L Alexander—just like the river that flows through its pages is one of the great treasures/sources that nourished and still nourish the literature of America.

I love to read to empower my inner self and understanding of the world outside.

It is common sense that everybody likes to write in humanity. It is a good faculty. Nobody minds this timeless elegance. To my brothers and sisters, we have an alliance with each other to keep and rely on one another as we save ourselves and humanity. Like John Paul II said, *As the family goes, so goes the nation, so goes the whole world in which we live.* Brothers and sisters we are each other's most resilient support and we dovetail together despite all collusion in the family. A family divided among itself would not withstand. It is survival of the fittest. We have each other to prosper together by the powers vested in God.

Write comprehensively. Topic sentence, supporting details and closing remark. Write the essay/work in as many paragraphs as you want as long as you tell everything you want the audiences to know. Practice is perfect.

Have space for writing. Background music is not recommended for full concentration. Think before you begin penning. Write one sentence a time and make sure it is coherent. Don't jump to different topics in a section/paragraph. It just takes time for your writing to gain elegance and to have style. Time will only move forward so continue practicing and you will progress. Worry about regressing? Then practice all the time to make sure you think fast when it comes to prehensile/*anchor* ideas for topics or urges.

Legibility in Writing: Check for spelling, grammar, coherency and make sure your sentences make sense.

Elegance/Style in writing: Write different sentence lengths to have emphasis in what you are trying to convey. Write with eloquence/voice.

Readership in writing: Reread your articles and make amends on your own.

Editing: Someone else can check your work to ensure 100% accuracy before publishing.

Discretion and care: Our team are learners and entrepreneurs/*businessmen*. We are fastidious learners and any learning is proactive, but we are not proactive at securing capital/*money* and are not wealthy as the entrepreneur businessmen. Those who value learning and knowledge are empowered in a smart and intelligent manner compared to those in the business world who are empowered by the power of money vested. Which ranks supreme? Knowledge or Money? Money is secondary in line after knowledge.

Our family conjoined both the learners and the entrepreneurs, brothers and sisters to make up this legal course that would encapsulate both learning and business. What would calm the disquietude at Court is the voice of reason. Any transaction needs reason vested, that is the main drive of life.

Consult us about vocalization and we will place you in the speaking tiers that best fits based on your eloquence.

Beginner: Speaker can utter with minor hiatus but utilizes lay and commonplace vocabularies to explain. Their speech is not as fast compared to advance and the tier above. Most people fall under this category and will advance with practice.

Advance: Advance speakers are more extravagant with their quotidian vocabularies, and are able to explain procedures. Fast speaking compared to beginners.

Expert: An expert speaker is an orator; an individual with the highest acumen in speaking and public speaking. Able to speak in front of a general audience without anxieties.

Remember don't be indolent and lackadaisical when it comes to speaking to people. Use your tongue of fire to articulate like the 12 disciples of Jesus. They were missionaries to heraldry and harbinger Jesus's teaching across the earth and soon there are now approximately 1.2 billion Roman Catholics. They were given strength from the holy spirit to overcome their anxieties to speak and make Jesus's words be widespread. They were able to recruit many converts with their tongue of fire to enlist and believe in his resurrection and finally there will be judgment day that is the end of the world. These missionaries are great orator.

Are you convinced? Life is about reason. Humanity has reasons to live for. All is fair in love and war. Life is fair and everything happens for a reason. There is godspeed/*fortunate*.

It is human nature to adjudicate reasons for human existence other than the insane. Why we are here is to full-fill our legacy which is to honor and respect our parents and live happily. Why we are here is to better our family and community eventually. To continue preserving the earth for the next generation while living on it and it's never about the destination but a journey. Growth and learning in any faculty transpires incrementally. Start your journey now and learn.

Speaking takes the most time to acquire. People take a whole lifetime to acquire and learn the art of articulation.

What is a long/lengthy word? Sesquipedalian

What is the longest word you know? antidisestablishmentarianism. The opposite of the disestablishment of the Church of England.

We will see, know, love.

A WHITE MASTERPIECE and Other Novellas

A White Masterpiece

FOREWORDS

Carol writes the words of her Grandpa while dealing with voices and loss of privacy. Brightwood is the land she imagined and dwells at to escape the voices and do her training in writing. She continues to socialize to revamp her speaking and reading avidly.

The sinew/*the parts of a structure, system, or thing that give it strength or bind it together* in me continued to live on of my Grandpa and I passed it along to the next generation. There isn't an instant that we do not know that we are being looked after by our ancestors in heaven. This is a blessing because when we encounter a predicament we know we are not alone but have guidance from our ancestors.

It was only before time that I realized the truth of matters that under no circumstances shall I let any obstacles barricade me and can get passed. No matter how obstructive the voices or hallucination becomes I can overcome it with the sinew bestowed by my Grandpa. With my Grandpa I have the bravado to make anything in life be undaunting. They cannot empower me with the sinew as my Grandpa since I discovered him. With the sinew that is discovered I find out there are answers to any unresolved questions. He is my guide. He guides me in life and in my career in writing and I am to pen the words of my Grandpa.

Early spring was once again in the aria I can hear the passerines' songs flutter and subtend its flock in the high acme. I was cosseted along the shade of the elm tree. I am not worried this time I have my Grandpa and I was the figure beneath the shade of its grove. The protagonist. He had passed the sinew onto me which is the gift of family. It has been a halcyon/*happy* day when I was admiring the weather and I had realized the brilliance of the vernal weather. It was one fine day when the greenery had been soothing and soporific. I was at the scenic natural resort where the weather was prefecture for perusing literature. I had laid over a blanket on the grass. There was serenity and here I was lavishing the charm of the aria efflorescence with spring's flora. The aria was all quiet and soporific when I had passed on the book and basked in idle watching the different shapes of clouds drifting in the sky. Somehow I had felt the clouds close by as though I was leaping a siesta on the cloud. The moisture on the grass was sifting through my back when I felt a cold down my torso. Then I ascended and strolled along the encircling of white color of Anna's Promise rose.

The scent of spring was in the air until the radiation was causing me to heat up and then I had to once again shield myself along the shade of the elm tree. Then I rested again because the soporific air put me on a siesta. It was close to an hour before I had opened my eyes again and I noticed that the afternoon was elapsing. There were now more chirping of the wrens and my sleep was golden. If the day could have just been like this without distractions of voices that would take our attention from tranquility.

It had felt like this sometimes the previous night before and I had time to revive myself after the writing piece. The night previous there had been a storm. Just last night I had felt the sensorium coming forward when I had been in contact with what seems like the underground and the celestial. There had been nothing else, nothing greater but I had sensed pain from the voices.

There is heraldry of spring and the sprinkle of rose petals in the air as though we had accomplished and yes indeed we have made it in my memories. When we had returned to see a different aria to notice that the season had changed from the winter hiemal to spring. To start another chapter of our life and this time it is the real event. When time passed we couldn't return to it again. We have cherished our time now. Sometimes we return to being a different person than we were. It has been 30+ years. It would be gone as I had hoped it would never be gone and the anima passes by in any way unceaseless, closer to my Grandpa. I am closer to the sky than I had ever been seen here and I am able to envision distal all the movements and transportation happening outside where there is great scatter of light and by the hour I hear the loud tumult of the train engine passing by this direction that had departed now. I feel the wind coming over this way where I had been in the lull. There again goes the sound of the train it had reserved and passed off. Now there were many trees seen while I was still doing training in my writing.

When I had wanted to perceive the city with the sound running over it. I had closed the window and kept myself focused inside. Each morning there were enough of the city then it had become chaotic hearing the sounds of traffic that I had enclosed myself in here. Though, there had been a lot of light outside. A little later, the train had passed and now I had been inside and I had needed to take a break. I would open the window to let the fresh air in when it had been a good day. Sometimes I had needed the window open so that it would block out some of the noises on the inside or if the outside had been intrusive I had remembered back then when I had been around people such were days of simple. Simplicity means happiness.

By noon time the sun was out and a little of the heat was felt through the window. Then I start to hear the wren named James chirping momentously the last remainder of summer. The weather is going to welcome autumn when it can be the best time of year. As though I was called out to nature they had replied with their hearkening. It couldn't be this but I sensed autumn. There were rattling machines and portents of men. It seems perfect that I can stay in the rest of the day and not have to go out. I didn't like it much where there was pollution and pesticides. It didn't take me long to get used to the environment, most of it is very fitting. Where the city was, had been pestiferous, why had it been this? This was the city where they encountered and departed anytime like the soundings of the train. This was better because I had been training myself to write and not deal with what was happening on the outside. They almost never get to see me out and I feel I wasn't contributing. Is that the purpose of being here? Well, I hadn't done much for this Earth but I didn't have to leave it in pollution. This place was not a nice Lake altogether. I had figured it out while there might even be the bad guys loitering.

In the evening there was still rage in the city, but a little cooler air had brought over the city and homes. There might be the last rage of the day. It was nearing the end of day and the tension outside had subsided, especially on Monday when the engine is still running another four days of the week. This hour the train sends the last round, they might be going out there to dinner at 7 o'clock now. Where had the time gone, that the day had taken place and almost done this evening when I was returning, stuck on a pointer. I quickly returned upstairs and resumed at my computer when the problem was no longer puzzling. Up here was clear. I can hear my own echoes when I let out a scream to subside the tension.

Where are the birds now? The birds settle on the railing during the day and anytime now it might freely elope into the air anywhere there is atmosphere. I wonder where the birds went and perhaps to the side of the world across here. I had seen it, flew distance someplace else now on the East, back then was on the West. How far would they be in a month? When will they be home? When will I be home? All day I had been inside and depicted some knowledge and understanding of today's world that scientifically explains it.

There was much moisture in the air; this was not much indiscretion. It feels like an oasis and I can see my reflection through the glass. This point was like the appearance of a vitreous edifice. I was here imbibing the nature of inspiration and absorbing my last hour of study. I feel myself submerged in the bath at the waterfall and looking out to see the freshness of nature like the clear water of the swamp and there were trees of varying size and heights that you can imagine.

I was blocking out sounds and voices. Irrelevant sounds so that we wouldn't enjoy life as much! I screamed out to the boulders and they might shake in fiery. They cannot beat us when our will is iron.

Brightwood is the land on the other side of the world. I would be here or imagine it to myself whenever I would come across the problem of the voices. Most of this place you're not going to see along with the people living. There was a lot of nature in the surrounding of multiple colors, a field of not much dour/*unfriendly* and amiable. A place where I imagined myself to rest from the voices. There were tree's variety assortments of different breeds. You smell the efflorescence and pick one out of all of them. This type of rose, the most ideal and superior breed, the white masterpiece. It is not this concisely supreme I shall say because you are in the garden not in the study room or space for chances that there might be something daunting and a black dragon might jump at you. My Grandpa is the golden dragon that fights it. This land did not exist, it was only in my imagination. I had stopped imagining when it was winnow except we weren't fighting uncertainty to be Rambo like machines and mammals. I had stopped short here whenever there was the roaming and roaring of the machine. I need to rest and recuperate in this place, the most effective antidote. I was able to get good lighting in this space. They were natural lights and not artificial. I must need them this afternoon just in case that the scatter stops and the gloom starts to come over. I can be found most of the time and I dwell all day here while I was doing my studies. One day I learned how to write fiction in all of this place.

Brightwood is a location I had spoken of where there were chances of fresh air that wasn't in synchronized with the air outside the city. It was a place in the back of my house where I got to go during break time to breathe. The houses were lit at night when the hour came to light it and by the nightfall there were lights sporadically on the hills. Sometimes the temperature might drop low enough that the top of the versant/*mountain* is covered in snow and its whiteness glows in the darkness of night. Some nights it never gets dark because we were too close to the starry sky and we saw the galaxy and orbits at the constellations. While there was life on Earth I was able to feel and breathe the cool air. There is better air up here than down there.

The people down there got to see the prosaic/*commonplace* activities though the ones more closed off had the house up at higher elevation. Every evening I return to the house and out of Brightwood when work is done. We take good care of ourselves and the time we have. It all makes sense by chance I was at the right place. I might go to Brightwood in the evening and share the fresh air there and be reminded of the serene environment that evening and then enjoy the rest of the night at the garden. This place was lit like a fresh spring. I can see the movement of water sometimes on stagnant paintings when I must have imagined it. I was able to hear the sounds of water billowing inward. It is refreshing. Water has other emblems of beauty but we hadn't wanted to recall this. It has personal conflict and tears. It was not yet time to light the lights the sun was beginning to set. The day was descending to adieu. The city was clearing out as the road was evacuating and was tepid by the night as we sequestered in our houses.

When I work late night in the study at Brightwood the pressure would build on. Evening hour the temperature had cooled and I had caught on signs of a few birds in the air. There are already more pollutants now than it had been earlier near closing hour. Now there is fresh air in the evening hour and I had sensed the tension alleviated in the air when the business buildings were closed and the homes were in use. Let in the fresh air now and be relieved of the insolence. I bear no burden and hold to my conviction that has been self-evident ever long term relentlessly until they have complied, those who have bent the truth. I refer to the voices. Perhaps not this fresh air they weren't applicable. Then they belong down there with the commoners. I saw the airplane flying overhead where there was good air and it was white light of hope! I had begun to see the light being light out. While my penning was still going on, my writing protracted this hour of night as the day was closing to the last dint. The city has begun to transform to night light when the lamppost was lit outside the street while I was giving my reminder efforts. I hadn't noticed when fresh air was sieving through the open window that the night was ending. I had seen the beginning of the day now when the day was closing, I had thought upon the passing hours that I had spent on my script, penning the words of my Grandpa when there was to be perfection.

Does God perceive us as we are? I'm sure he does.

MEETING OF THE PATRIARCH

With its long history filled with complications and hardships, the patriarch had endured, my Grandpa is the sinew of the country. It needs strong leadership to revamp the economy and rebuild it up after the war. The men of the household are discussing the best means to solve this complication at a meeting. The patriarch sits aside pensively, lighted a special cigarette and listens to the congregation speak. He observes the men discussing the issues in their unit and speaks up to make a decision after hours elapsed. Discussions and voting would take place.

It wins unanimous. The family is to go.

"Grandpa Phu, I know they must all go," said the houseboy. There was rain and thunder. "When will they be back?"

"Long I think. The journey is long," said Grandpa Phu. "I hope they all make it. There are traps and snares I am afraid for some. The second I admonished.

"What mishaps can there be?"

"The road meanders, we never know. There are trials and some errs." He sighed. "Run along now, we must prepare them."

We are a Catholic family and believe in Jesus as our savior. The family prays together every Saturday before we convene for dinner. We live by the words of

Jesus and Grandpa is like Jesus. He will bestow on us goodness if we pray to him. We are all very religious.

Every member of the family is a central character. When my Grandpa passed away we couldn't take it because he was the main character and our sinew. Our seven siblings were pillars that were established and inculcated. How we understand wisdom to be wise and never condone mistakes. We would amend them and try our best not to err.

God's precepts are Grandpa Phu's rules. We shall never violate the ten commandments.

1) You shall have no other gods before me
2) You shall not make more yourself an idol
3) You shall not misuse the name of LORD your god
4) Remember the sabbath day by keeping it holy
5) Honor your father and your mother
6) You shall not murder
7) You shall not commit adultery
8) You shall not steal
9) You shall not give false testimony against your neighbor
10) You shall not covet

We shall talk of number seven. You shall not commit adultery. Grandpa Phu does not want anyone of us to have premarital sex. He says it contaminates the world. This generation the young adults are more liberal therefore they should know. This we must condone.

I am set out to finish Grandpa Phu's commission to write a novel appertaining to what Grandpa Phu says. I believe that he is still living in me. From gray to white were his years of patriarch. His hair when I saw him last had been gray and now it had turned white after 5 years and enigmatically somehow, he must have grown 6 feet.

A White Promise

"Love and War."

"There will be hope."

I first told of my timeless experiences when I have been building in the process of my inner self.

Time spins in a round clock engirdled in full circles without beginning or end till the coming of age and continuum. Time is urgent, rushed and indispensable before time runs out. There is only a rush for second place.

Timelessly, not affected by passage of time or lasting, known for all times. Timeless is ad libitum, endless, without beginning or end.

First is the development of the conscience as it has been caducous and as we venture on the journey of life that is disposed of, even before the development of personality and self-identity; for life is harrowing and stricken and an endangered denizen. This self-actualization is altered because of experiences and it can be a breach. This is what happened to Lux Aeterna; the antagonist of the novel. *Requiem of a Dream.* Was this all a dream that happened to Lux? He will effaced it in four phases of the lepidoptera that look into his conscience and find guiding light. This is prosaic about humanity to find redemption.

Is this a love book or a war book? Both love and war entwined. The protagonist Wian Brown is conflicted by his feelings for his wife which is the love part in the novel whether to incarcerate his brother in law, the crux of the problem. The infamous Lux combated Wian Brown in the war of prestigiousness, prodigious, and power and in the end to win Alice's heart.

While he should have been more understanding, not just caring and lenient towards his older sister Alice and not let anger seize him like in the killing of the lepidoptera from internal cohesion. Had Lux been more thought out the accident could have been expunged/*erased*.

We do not pick Lux because of his provenance/*origin*. As background, he was remedial while going to school and slow. When he grew up he dispensed with language acquisition problems and endured hallucination. This pained him that he is not able to make connections compared to Wian verbally. Lux is a fob. Though, he is emotionally perceptive or conative to Alice. He has a profundity of thoughts though his weakness is that he is not able to say it or as eloquent as Wian.

Maybe this has taken place the course of this winter time, when the setting happens Wian Brown has been on the chronometrical awaiting for his brother in law Lux to return from the preadventure that would formulate his character to be incarcerated on his will. When he gets out of prison they will begin anew, talabu rasa, but this time the chase has ended.

"Are you here to incarcerate yourself? asked Wian. "There was never a doubt that you'll get here now. Get ready. Get set to go in there. The verdict is ten years.

I will wait for you. When you are released as I had promised Alice." said Wian.

"I entrust you. I knew I should have before because I know you love Alice and so do I. I'm sorry. There is nothing else left that I can say, but I truly am destroyed and hurt. I should never have attempted to hurt you. Please give me another chance." said Lux.

Wian looked down but disgusted at Lux. But then he remembered his last promise to his wife Alice. "You have erred and done indelibly wrong to me. Just take care of yourself. Go now."

"I'm an imbecile," admitted Lux as he succumbed in complete remorse.

"Serve your sentence. I have nothing to tell you until you are out," said Wian solemnly.

Time elapsed in silence and Wian occasionally visited Lux in recidivism.

Nine years later…

It is the ninth year anniversary of Alice's death. Wian visited Alice's grave at the Dignity Memorial. The black gate in celestial surroundings seemed as though Wian was walking through heaven. You'll never regret attending a funeral. But there were many regrets Wian upheld before Alice's last words. He wished he had more time with Alice. He remembered her smile. The brim of her lips would contour in happiness when riant smile. All he wanted was for her to be happy. He knew he had made her a white promise. But there was not a chance that Lux could have escaped imprisonment. Incarcerating Lux was the rightful act and decision over Alice's will to acquit him. This is the judgment.

These are his musings. Today I visited Lux and already it has been nine years. I hope Lux has changed and gained in character. Though I still despised our brother vehemently. I don't understand why you have to depart from our life...which now is a new beginning for me. I never thought I could be without you and life is just as difficult as that.

"So how are you now Lux?" inquired Wian.

"Not so good brother in law. Though I do hope one day I can return again. My strength is growing weaker by the day. Some days I fall ill and I thought I might never awake again," said Lux.

"Let your soul rest. I will devote an orison to you."

The next morning there lay the golden sun with red stretta above the horizon. There is cranium ascending at dawn. There is orison for intelligent passion. There is hope.

Visions of Wian Griffit Brown

"Wian has two main schisms: family and debonair. Like love and money, respectively."

"How does Wian, the mason, build a skyscraper? By his Character."

Every day starts new responsibilities at Debonair Sanatorium. Wian entrance through the vitreous door of Debonair Sanatorium and yesterday closed behind him.

Wian is accompanied by Lincoln Timer, his handyman, the second indispensable schism of Wian besides Alice. Lincoln is his most proximal helper among the other medical cadre/*entourage*. His right hand man.

When is the perfect timing? Lincoln is the man that keeps check and hussles Wian that time is potent. Again sometimes time is ad libitum. But for a proactive and productive man like Wian, time is always on the run. Seldom does he have time spares to be languorous/*idle*. When that is, he is often still around Lincoln, his watcher of time while sojourning at Debonair Sanatorium all day. Lincoln Timer is the man who keeps track of his schedules and appointments.

Debonair Sanatorium is Wian life's project along with his family which are his most special destinies. He is the owner of the hospital and built it into a skyscraper. How much does it take to construct a skyscraper? It is a measure of a man's whole life efforts and smartness. It takes an extensive amount to build a skyscraper. It requires him to be prolific in the course of this time in his performance to save up, the man of talent and success is cognizant. The skyscraper is expensive.

Wian builds it to be an exceptional place. Debonair is magnificent in structure with its tapering minaret and bulbous dome. It is incisive and never random, but there are aleatory/*chances* that are God's doing through Christopher Wren. The vitreous is beaming against the sun ray and the frit is admirable and iridescent. There is amiable good verve and out are signs of Christopher Wren against the looming of the structure. The skyscraper is situated at good feng shui. Wian is sensible to every verve, breath, anima, he sees his success a distance alluring in the sky, sights of the looming skyscraper. At this time there is hammering and rattling of the masons reconstructing the shattered skyscraper where Lux had inflicted a shot.

Wian is the man of judgment along with the present Judge of here, Judge Beth. He has appointed Debonair into excellent order. Debonair is a place of senses and reasons, prevailing judgements, status and sophistication, diversity, differentiation, and self-delineation.

Wian surpasses many stunts, nothing can get in the way and hampers him. Wian is a man of his words. A highly intelligent individual who can give any order a say, an impeccable man of judgment instinctively. He does not let himself be ambivalent and does not vacillate once he makes a decision. His words are orders. On the professional side, he is a confidante to the cadre and an advisor. Personally, teachers to the twin girls Einstein and Charmaine, Adam and the dearest loving husband of Alice.

Wian always survives pass the stunts and this time again. There are operations every day that starts with renascence/*rebirth* and he surpasses all of them. Never is there an error in judgment. Wian has many gray hairs because of natural graying. He is a profound thinker. Wian is a man of thought. Very well thought out before any actions. Words are power just as much as actions are prone. He is more than a great ideal doctor, in appreciation to his father. He is not a typical airborne doctor but he is a man of thinking while most doctors cannot think. Wian is differentiated and has clear intelligence and is a loving soul. He is a man of good judgment and character.

Wian is a vigilante. The sole goodness of the world. He is a proponent of the world and life. A truly good person. Wian is the reason amidst madness. He is ordered among chaos that everything else needs to have… reason.

DEBONAIR

Wian's faithful student Adam Clive was on the way to the sanatorium. Also his adopted son. Adam has one more year remaining of training at the hospital before he can become a psychiatrist. Adam has been dealing with the symptoms of hallucination which is when you hear and see delusional things and noises that are not present but the brain perceives it as present. This symptom is called hallucination.

Adam has been a tantamount assistant to Wian in the help of researching Lux's symptoms. Lux had been hallucinating, which caused him to attack the sanatorium close to a decade back. Wian had still been looking into Lux's diagnostic to help Lux extricate/*disentangle* the imposition that had left him to foray the hospital. Wian had devised several analyses to why Lux had been incapacitated and which madness drove him to the shooting. He had found testimony while putting Lux on arraignment in prison of the possible neural pathways that had led him to his insane action to foray the sanatorium and victimized Alice but with premeditated intention of killing Wian. Wian the man of reason is searching amidst the testimony of Lux's madness. So that Wian can cure Lux's psychopath.

It has been nine years and they have done several interviews to see if he is better for early bailing out of prison but Lux is still found to be incapacitated and self-deprecation and guilty for killing Alice, his beloved sister. Lux cannot forgive himself for abducting the life of his most beloved. His compunction/*conscience* leads to break down and needs further recovery. As promised to Alice, Wian awaits Lux when he gets out of prison.

"Has it been torture Lux? It is time you can get out if you want but the sentence can be served for one last year. Do you have any wishes at this time"

"Do you think I am cured? I don't trust myself compared to you."

"What impelled your actions to act? I meant the shooting with intent to kill me?" Wian guffawed.

"I shouldn't have at all, brother in law. I was young and arrogant. I was also manipulated. Alexander, that bastard tricked me to vie you. But what truly impelled it was because I am weak. I am tenuous. I gave into his flattery. I was arrogant and wanted cynosure. That dog tricked me with his flattery."

"Alexander has not been arrested, he is nowhere to be found."

"It is absurd, everyone is against your cynosure. I am sorry. It even perturbed me."

Wian guffawed again. "Let's go visit Alice before the end."

Lux fell ill the day Wian had asked the jurisdiction for release to a visit of the cemetery. Wian was given the fiat/*authority* to drive the prisoner to the

22

cemetery and sought the deceased victim. Lux fell down on the tombstone crying aloud and endless.

"I deserve death, Alice, for doing this to you. I am very very sorry. I don't deserve anything. Don't blame Wian," Lux said crying aloud and then sobbing after hours. "I remember when we were young and you gave everything and saved everything you had for me until Wian came. I owe you my life. Of course Wian is good, like yourself. Both juristic. What would I do? I lack guidance when I am a risk taker to be a hustler. I wanted to be there sooner than everybody. I know I am not as honest as you. You were so pure with a kind heart. How could I have?" And he broke down crying again.

Alice riant beautiful smile shown from a distance in heaven looking down at them. There were puffs of clouds that drifted in the sky that looked like heart shapes and images of Alice seemed transparent in Wian's head. Wian shed a tear from the brim of his eyes.

*   *   *

Returning to contemporary, this is the replete event of the foray.

"How do you cure a psychopath?" Wian Brown has seethed to fix this when the topic is at debate. Wian sees they connived for all of this to happen. They wanted to kill him for cynosure. It is the methodology of the psychopath. They had planned to attack the sanatorium and the bulbous dome hospital was shattered at the scene of the shooting. Lux had forayed the hospital with intent on killing Wian but Alice had been there and intercepted his attack. He had a gun hidden and no one knew through the security cameras when he walked in because he was one of the doctors at Debonair.

Lux navigated through the corridors well when no one was watching him and sought Wian, but coincidentally Alice was present. Lux wanted to catch Wian when he was alone. It was around 11 am in the morning when they heard a gunshot at the sanatorium. It was a loud gun shot that startled everyone present. Sounds like a loud crack and a bang. One shot had missed Wian and pierced the wall of the skyscraper sanatorium and caused a shatter. Sent out timorously to the crowd who were in blockage and hiding behind tables and cots in the patient's room. Lux had found Wian close to his personal office but the second shot he tried to get Wian was a shock when his sister Alice intercepted and the shot hit her upper torso close to the atrium. Lux was in terror when he saw his sister coming in the way but he couldn't stop the shot. The shot dispensed from the rifle at a fast pace going directly at Wian but Alice had intercepted. "NO!!!" Lux cried out when he saw Alice. At that moment he wished he had not aimed the shot to hit Alice. She immediately fell back and dropped to the ground in Wian's arms. The moment he saw Alice, Lux was discontented. He did not want that to happen. He wanted to intercept the shot. Both Lux and Wian saw the shot coming and impaled Alice's body. Lux was taken away by the policeman who arrived at the scene of the crime roughly in minutes when someone triggered the emergency alarm. A convoy of police vehicles

24

arrived at the sanatorium to arrest Lux. But Lux escaped with extenuating circumstances and promised to be back.

The sanatorium was left in dismal before 12 noon to the tenebrous tiding of Alice's dying. Alice laid in Wian's arm and whispered her last breath.

"Please don't die," cried Wian. Knowing something bad is happening. "I am not going to let you die on me like this Alice."

"Don't Wian dear...I want you to promise me something Wian," Alice said in pain grasping her breath. "I want you to help Lux get acquitted so that he would not have to go to prison... I know it was not his intention to shoot. Please Wian."

Wian sobbed and was overwhelmed with tears. "He must pay if the law bides Alice. This is awful. No Alice. No... Your brother is a bastard. I don't know what to do. He must pay Alice. I do not want the law not to arrest Lux for starting this collusion. I don't know how he had conspired the shooting." Wian continues to sob and cry aloud. Whining to Alice that she must be fine and copacetic.

"It is my fault for neglecting him. He had told me complaints about you and I totally disregarded it to pick your side. I would never believe that Lux would do this to harm you. He told me you were astringent. You always had your eyes on him as some insect that would ruin it for everybody."

"And here he is shooting at the hospital to start such wreckage…" Wian cried like a baby in colic and frustrated. Your brother is nothing but a kid, a fool who cannot adjust himself better. He deserves prison if there are justifications to all of this. I am strict. But not an asshole like Lux. I only make sure to watch over him and that gets him whizzy and uneasy. He is a maniac. I'm so sorry Alice. All this has to happen. If not then you wouldn't be in this condition and I only protect you. "

"It is alright dear. I know you mean well. Lux does not like someone watching over him. Please mean well for Lux too."

"Well he is a fool and needs to be watched over. I know not to trust him without supervision. Defying order is madness and your brother is a maniac to foray this attack and matters at hand are not well. He'd sacrifice you Alice. I am justified authority, not some whimsical fiat. He is jealous of my cynosure. The fool doesn't know how to act and his words are empty. Just don't listen to what he says until he has made some growth and done building my dear. I hate that bastard all the time!"

Alice groaned in pain. "I hope I can live to see that day when he is built." She coughed. "I love my brother dearly and please don't let anything bad happen to him. Please promise me. You will take care of him when I am not around. I must go soon. I love you dear, most. Please don't cry "

"Alice no…please don't go and give up. Don't

relinquish us. I love you Alice."

"Please promise me... Wian, to take care of Lux and yourself as well."

"I'm sorry my dear. I promised," he replied.

"Thank you. Thank you again. You are a good man to me. Please keep the promise. I'm sorry too. I must go." Alice spoke her last breath. And rest her eyes.

"I white promise you my dear. Rest assured." She kissed him one last time with her last breath. Then Alice passed away in Wian's embrace. Wian let out a cry of dramatic pain. Louder like the gun shot. One that is piercing and everlasting. For a second it seems like time had stopped when he was speaking with Alice. Alice had been a sweetheart. His one and only kiss. Tears inundated Wian and overwhelmed him. And no matter what he could not stop crying. It was automatic and by default. He could not hold his tears back. There was silence while Wian kept crying and then the convoy of policemen came to console Wian.

"It is a tragedy. I'm sorry for Misses Brown death." said the police

"Where is Lux? He is going to pay! You killed my wife!" shouted Wian.

"He gave extenuating circumstances, and he said he will come back."

"I will surely get him back. I know the bastard will come back!"

"We trust you. We are not going to send a search for him and await the time when he gets back then."

Lux's extenuating circumstance is his medical condition and Alice's last words to let him free. The sanatorium was at the scene of timorous/*fear* and closed down for the rest of the day. They were not admitting patients for the day because of the disaster. The bulbous dome skyscraper was shattered and they had to send in maintenance and repair to do the fixing. The repair of the structure was not difficult but the reputation of the place had to be renewed and reestablished. There were rumors of shooting and that brought timorous to the patients and visitors and people shunned the place at first. When the news of the shooting was first promulgated many permanent visitors inquired about it to discover the inside of it and what happened to the renowned doctor Brown and his wife. The news was kept reticent and only to the family of the Brown.. Although it was promulgated on the news tersely about the death of Dr. Brown's wife.

Wian tried to get everything back to normal having put a kibosh on it. Something parallel to what is going on in the auric field perpetuates in the appurtenances space outside. He roved outside to make observations of the quagmire and see how it is happening. He can observe from the infrastructure of the vitreous skyscraper the hospital building of Debonair shattered.

The news is out this morning. Wian worked this morning and was accosted by traffic. He doesn't want to cry being by himself. The statue stood gray against the skyline as appurtenance to the quayside by the bay. On the left is the obsidian skyscraper. Debonair is located on the right venue of the railing. In critical timing, it is black. There are the other industrialized buildings he can see as miniatures when he drives across the bridge. From the sanatorium he can see it as well. They are looming of various heights. How many of us rest here at termination of a day when the recourse/*options* can no longer be worse only to find a breeze of fresh air by going to the railing. The aria is good here and a positive place to end a day. Then returning to his habitat that is now shattered any sequential details can happen. He watches out often for other mishaps. Aleatory, the hospital is a safe place.

It has been nine years now and just now he has sensed something dismal in the atmosphere. Lux had been working at the hospital not long ago. Wian had been suspicious of Lux to be the culprit. There is enough devise and tinges from innumerable throb of anguish to stubbornly twist them into a curse that he better be censured. The obstinate tide the previous times the dark power of the magnate had been left to arise. He must have sensed the collusion. They have abetted and Lux is incarcerated. Alexander the jeweler had been fined and lost touch from this society. Their places are out of Debonair. Wian never wants to see them again. Lucky Lux has his sister who infiltrated to acquit him, still he is sentenced. The verdict is only a decade in prison and he has surceased/*stopped*.

Wian walks along the railing as the carmine sun is casting its silhouette ubac/*the shady side of the mountain* onto the bay. The ubac is before the adret/*the mountainside that faces the sun.* Lux is the ubac. The adret is disappeared after vesper when the sun descends behind the stratus cloud. No one is there. It had been spooky overnight and low resolution soundings of Lux infiltrated the walls when he angered from last night. Lux attacked him at the sanatorium and coincidentally Alice Aeterna was there and intercepted. They affrayed/*attacked* and she had been shot by accident.

The atmosphere distilled until the next morning when the first spectre of light effused and he felt worse. It is the first day without Alice. He has to sequester to the sanatorium he contemplated, but for security the fiat closed the sanatorium; it is going to be closed until it is safe to re-administered. His compartment is shut down. The jurisdiction evacuated the compartment to assure of safety. There are people needing investigations and testimony. The authorities and objects are there at the scene of the crime. Wian Brown has been present and his license is inspected ephemerally. The jurisdiction has commiseration of Wian Brown deceased amative/*mate.* They urged him to tarry/*stay* home to find placate. Wian insisted on tarrying the hospital. He wanted to rescue her in the emergency. Wian Brown tried to resuscitate but her condition is detrimental. The cadre hospitalized Alice in the emergency room and she passed away. She was shot near the atrium by the criminal. He shot two sporadic bullets. It damaged the vitreous. She does not survive. The aim was at Wian.

There have been shots and damages to the inside. The frit of one compartment vandalized and exposed from the outside. Some of the frit shattered and the bullets made perforation in the walls. There is security going in and out of the hospital to ensure the patients safety. He has to give heed to the pernicious condition.

Debonair has to rebuild the opacity of its damage. The construction has been initiated to repair the foray from the bullets. Wian ordered the construction to initiate immediately and the sanatorium to return to its original. He appoints the installation without hesitation. Debonair has been Wian's life grand project and hard work. He has to be stationed until order resumed and the compartment is renovated to safety. Debonair has made reparation for autotelic/*having an end to a purpose itself* and arrivederci/*hello*. They divulged Alice's death that made a tremendous effect on him. His license is returned and he is allowed to practice again after consulting with the jurisdiction. The jurisdiction/*police* wanted to know why he was the aim of the shooting and why he was the motive. What astirred Lux's motive to shoot Wian? They wanted his testimony although they know he is cynosure and prestigious. It was protocol. The Judge that administered the casual arraignment of Wian is Judge Beth.

"What do you think is Lux's motive? What perpetuated his actions?" inquired Judge Beth happily that she gets to speak with Wian.

"Lux returned from medical school only about

five years ago after his residence in a different region to work with me, referred to by his sister, the victim. I wasn't always fond of him because of his abruptness of personality and false ruthlessness towards those needed than family. He is not discrete in his work and personal. Not a man of his words cannot be trusted that I discovered over time working with him. He can be a flake."

"What were you doing the day of the shooting? Why do you think Lux has to rid you?"

"I will tell you all about it. That day of the shooting I was in my office with Alice. I had my back turned and then the next second I realized there was a gun shot that hit the skyscraper window and then Alice got in front of me suddenly and there was another gun shot and it had hit Alice. Lux was appalled and ran out of there. Alice mentioned before that Lux didn't like that I was astringent to him. He is allergic to authority and didn't like being watched. On the contrary, he wants authority for himself. But Lux is pretense, when he is administration at watch. You can never tell verisimilitude in his words. That pisses me off."

"Where do you think he is now Wian? I greatly appreciate your testimony."

Wian sighed. "Where can Lux be? He is in hiding because of what he has committed. I know he will return for Alice's funeral. Lux is not a bad character when it comes to loving his sister that is what I had not minded him from the beginning. He was a good brother to my wife."

"I comprehended. That is when we will take Lux then. For now let him be on the loose. You know what I think?" She sighed. "People do wrong and are delinquent because they don't have everything they need. They want more power, crave for power then what they have got. It leads them to jealousy, being less and do destruction to others to hamper them. Only the psychopath doesn't get it. There are plenty of good people out there as there are bad people. We would lose you the most prodigious over some maniac if Alice had not intercepted. She did well. I can't believe he would ever act out as this"

"Very disappointing. He will be there with Alice. I promised. Thank you, your honor. Wian said gratefully and happily. This is the first time since Alice passed away that Wian had been happy because he was praised.

"By the way, your honor, how did you know you were going to become a judge to celibate? Did you have nightmares? I used to have those dreams all the time and it would give me the chills because there was adrenaline from the post-apocalypse. Alice and I both had nightmares. We concluded that it might be judgment day foretold to us and we are meant to judge," asked Wian timid somewhat. He was trying to ingratiate himself.

"Maybe dear. Maybe judgment can just be nature. All humans can judge, they can judge badly. Not all have good judgments. This is why we have crimes. You and I are both people of good judgments. I'm not sure about those nightmares though. How are you doing with Alice gone? I share with you deep condolences. Husband I don't have, but losing a loved one I know is most grievances and heartfelt."

"There is a sense of oblivion and loss. I stare out into space not knowing where to find her again when the hour elapses. Alice is always chatting. I miss her embrace and charisma. The two twin girls make up for some loneliness."

"Indeed. See me if you ever need anything my dear Wian."

"I will. The world always needs someone with good judgment. I am glad we share the same interest, to eradicate injustices."

Amidst the intercity he does not want patients to be timorous of the shooting and tried to keep matters silent but the news was reported and they spoke of it on several channels.

The carmine sun is already up high and he can sense the execration/*cursing* at the beginning of the day. It seems cryptic though nothing effusive still at this bathetic/*anticlimax* hour quiescence. He is cognizant that the shooting occurred Alice had been moribund/*approaching death*. It has been dispersed on the news.

"There has been revolutionized. The victim's affiliation attempted insurrection against the suspect's brother-in-law, unwonted and the demise is poignant.

Alice Aeterna the victim demands full acquittal of her brother Lux. This is to go to trial and the victim's husband Wian Brown will decide the ultimate verdict. There is going to be further investigation of the paradox," said the reporter.

"The jurisdiction have given the suspect considered criminal extenuation labeled insane he does not want the label of homicide and will get back to us. Obstruct cognizant in the process to foray and affray his own affiliate is submitted to the sentence. With the insistent of acquitting before her last breath. We are prowling of susceptive evidences against his insanity. There has been doctor's consent. It is up to the brother-in-law," said the reporter.

Wian has been taciturn for a time with the condition of his wife and the sanatorium aspersion. His wife had been shot. Wian is agitated why she would acquit.

The massive show respect to the building not giving heed to the schematic traversing their profundity/*wisdom*. There is publicity of the skyscraper being destroyed and news of Alice's fantod/*unreasonableness*.

It is a while when the news is promulgated and the medical cadre hears that they resumed to work at their appointments. Wian knows chaotic and hope transience /*elapse* while he deals with Alice's catastrophe. The massive have incorporated for sanctioned and censured against the facility unsafe condition that they might administer.

Apropos/*with reference* to Alice body is carried to the mortuary to preserve for a time.

Wian knows her allegation of Lux. He would have to figure it out. Will Lux show at Alice's funeral if they held one now or where is Lux to be found? He needs to find Lux and beat the hell out of him.

Wian has Debonair on his mind. He knows he has opus/*work* to take care of. This diurnal day he has opus to work. He was distracted by Alice and sadness brood over him. He has calibrated that if it would be just for Alice's concern and abrogated it to care of Lux her murderer. He protested to himself. He would not be fine with the expiation/*atonement* if it meant acquit. Acquitting Lux would not mean retaliation and either way there is going to be debarred/*disentitled* for the incursion.

There is something dithering/*undecided* but she is not here anymore so he does not have to reconsider to her supposed last breath. It would be nearly absurdity if he is to submit there would be repercusion/*backlash*. The incurred sentence is adequate and incarceration is copacetic. There is meagerly inversion breeze when morning is carmine shines effulgently. Wian does not feel the carmine shine because it was going against his judgment that Lux must be punished.

Alice intercepted the shot to save him and he can not be relentless to her last wish, but he has to be de jure. At the scene her loser brother has been implacable and not watched of Alice. It would only affix if Lux incarcerated himself or enforced the sentence. Now Lux lost it and demised.

It could have been him demised and because of Alice he survived. He does not think it plausible to forgive Lux and Alice adjure/*request solemnly* to his release is antagonized and disproved. Lux must be in carceral if it is by predilection for her to be happy to make sense. It should have been and ought to be the way. He subject to Lux's peccavi/*guilt*. Alice has helped him and he felt not in the least obligated for this jurisdiction. It has been his decision and he does not think it perfidy/*untrustworthy* at attempt of her last breath. There would be perdure/*endure* of Lux's peccavi that he would have to execute. It would be his enforcement. He is implementing Lux's sentence. He does not have to implement it as criminal has to be convicted. Wian keeps musing on her last words and somehow he should care but himself would not let.

He would return rapidly to the hospital on purport and finish the appointments. There can be residue distillation on the side which has been obverse outside of Debonair. After convalescence he would spend time on schedule to ad hominem/*appealing to feelings rather than intellect* properly. By ad hominem he should wield to Alice but all reasons. Lux is served and sentenced.

The cadre of doctors does not think the shooting has been Wian's demerit/*fault*, but has he been teleology/*cause*? It has defamed comportment/*personality*. They are against his wife's will and not abide as well. There is humanitarian that the demean must be prosecuted and he is adhering to the laws. If Wian has no panache */self assurance/flamboyant* he would not get all the attention and maybe it would not get Alice shot. Perhaps the entourage has shown envious of his cynosure and abhorred his flamboyant that has been teleology/*cause* of the bitter attack. Wian is lamenting and they sought him in comfort. The cadre knows of Alice's sacrifice and the incident of the fiat collusion. They felt remorse for him. The news has been pervasive. When he is able to cogitate on his own space, situations would be right again and revamped. Wian thinks Alice is still alive and senses her apparitions. He sensed her *apparition* in the painting at the sanatorium later when he is in distress of her memories.

The clock tower in the intercity/*existing in the city* does not work. It was there in ancient compared to the beginning of the novel. What time is it now? Time is well spent and is meaningful with Alice and Wian. *I never juxtaposed you with Lux but look out.*

When we are ready we will be together again.

Lepidoptera One

"The lepidoptera caused internal cohesion
that agitated him overnight after dimmet and he
acted out and rid the incontinent."

The story of a murderer: the Lepidoptera

"Where is Lux?" screamed Wian and his
intonation is resounded across the terrain afar where
Lux recalled he once rusticated in anachronism. It
happened years ago when he told the story to Alice. He
once killed a lepidoptera overnight because of internal
cohesion to rid the continent. In the story he thought
he was a moth and it turned out he is a lepidoptera
murderer. Pabulum.

When the crime is committed, the city is out to
get him adversely and piercing darkness is brooding
over him from their covetous eyes. He must escape
from the riddling of life which is admonition/*warning* of
possible recrimination/*accusation* and the sides
interjected against him for having committed
machination/*stealing* of character. He lost his character
in a serious crime of lepidoptera murderer. In
contemporary times, the lepidoptera is the symbol of
Alice. Am I a truly a murderer? He talks to his
conscience of the event leading to the death of Alice.
Unaccepting that he is the killer and his own sister is the
victim.

There is the juxtaposed between light and dark
and furtherance the investigation of the killer has gone

on. Somewhere afar in rustication/*live in the countryside* his thoughts are sprawled into distal and his visage is seen through ratiocination. There is Lux in rustication in anachronism/*belonging to another time* when he reasoned these musings/*thinkings* to himself. He would not have to withhold his musings any longer until his escape and he is able to hear his own thoughts out.

Let the lepidoptera find light in darkness. Which is obscured intermittently, it is possible to see the picturesque/*attraction.* I am attractive, I am not a killer. It cannot be me.

The world is forlorn. If we are dissuaded from uncertainty, unprepared and dithering/*undecided.* The moth is the initiative or amateur that is the crux of the diurnal until there is satori/*enlightenment.* The silent plenum/*environment* in the nascent/*development* is where its latency/*beginning existence* has effector; the symbol of the lepidoptera.

First is the development of the conscience as it has been caducous/*shedding* and as we venture on the journey of life that has disposed even before the development of personality and self-identity; for life is harrowing and stricken/*trouble* and an endanger denizen. This self-actualization is altered because of experiences and it can be breach/*damage* in blunder.

On the contrary the way of performance, adjust our mind to become experienced. He has made mistakes somewhere and from his experiences he has new insights to revival. This recount is a journey through the musings that are embedded in the psyche.

How he reasons to condone himself the intent of a psychedelic/*psychopathic* killer and would repent the sins when he makes justification to himself that indeed he is to be decried/*publicly denounced.*

There is something query about the fabulation/*untrue of the musing* that he has to take precaution because of its unnerving consequences; that is, they fused thoughts to siege telepathic transmission which he never thought. He has mentioned it hallucination the system of theoretical depredation/*downfall.* This conceptual is being reiterated in the thought process, not truism but rather fabricated thoughts to alter emotions and the cause of cri de coeur/*passionate outcry.* It is incessant and he hopes that perforation would be terminal.

He thinks it emotional that Alice and him plighted/*promised* then it turned into a fight in the utterance of puerile/*childish* and frolicsome till flippant/*carefree* turned dire/*deadly.* He recalled images and flashbacks of Alice.

Lux does not know where to transgress from this beginning now. There is a profusion/*plenty* of thoughts in this mind that he exhumed/*dig up* from his phantom the scare that he lost it under the subjugation of the magnate. Alexander Tanner cannot pressure him to cause him dubious amidst his confidence at derisive. He is confident in the wreck that deluged. The deprecation/*disapproval* would defame him and there is no return now. Has Alice sacrificed and intercepted the shooting? Lux is dismal of her and he must return if he is the perpetrator. His thoughts have not been lucid and he despatched on extenuation before the musings divulged to make matters copacetic. He has to inspect matters with Alice.

To Alice he has always been with valor and dexterity in arms then he found the path to direct conscience and develop virtues. This is happiness and he has been revamped/*improved*.

Then he takes matter of rescind/*revoke* which he has been supple/*flexible*. He must reason it out to himself and not be exploited/*taken advantage* they would caliber every cost to multiply the damage of the sanatorium and injuries when he only redeems for which happens to his blood if anything happened.

The astringent would harbor him the suffocation anybody would urge retaliation against their fiat and authority. He would never go back there to the tiger or Wian Brown if it is not forced.

Alexander Tanner has been provoking him to kill Wian for cynosure. Lux has noticed solecism/*blunder* in the time that he has spent in solipsism/*solitude* because of collusion/*conspiracy* and the outside world is not accessible.

He thought of Alice when the thought of killing Wian crossed, there is now intricacy. He would have to handle her and she handles him. He thinks for himself and knows that he has exegesis/*explanation* to delineate. He does not think himself defiant. He has broken the law. It has been about breaking it down into pieces and then unraveling the parts one sector per sequence then its envelope can be analyzed at the microscopic level.

He has been looking at a tree full of leaves and its margent is visible to the naked eyes which without aspiration and passion has been reluctant and unattended to which he has not seen full details; in conjunction the spherical has been conglomerate and undifferentiated.

To which he has been observing from far away the landscape has never been ventured. He would never make the ascent and would never be an asshole to Alice. It has been all emergent and then one day he urges himself to closer observation and he looked into the envelope and the magic is discovered. He is making connections and seeing the labyrinth and every matter that it encompasses the way the universe operates. It is stemming and bricolage/*creation from a diverse range of available things*, it has been enigmatic though through other sources he is able to find out the place, the grand visage that has not been demean/*belittle*. He has to calibrate. He has been inanition from the miasmic/*stench* entangle of collusion against her significance and commination/*threatening vengeance* in which he has been brooding from the blithe/*careless* world that caused misjudgment where duplicity/*deceitfulness* can be pass for safe and impunity. Which he only has self-abnegation/*self-blaming* for whichever is extenuating there is none. I can't do this to Alice. She is way innocent, wait there is Wian. This would ever get pass him. She is my significance.

The storm has subtended and there is the turn of the next page. He understands the milieu and is

43

cognizant of his brotherhood and responsibility. He has hope that the dubiety would be indicted and sentenced. Last night he is befuddled by the double spirits that would not cease their banter/*mocking* so that he would not have his placation/*pacified* by being frigorific/*freeze* through the entire dimmet/*dusk*. The verbigeration/*noises* is interminable and while he bask/*sleep* the double takes his vigor the nocturnal energy that he harbors, dissipates to direct the negative energy in opposite in cri de coeur/*passionate outcry*. In number his indifferences have been obstructive of the silent plenum/*environment*; the Father has not believed in his sin nor would he possess in thinking Lux would ever perpetrate wrongly against Alice. No one would perpetrate against innocent Alice.

"Father I think I have the monster, I have to disable the musings that inundate," said Lux.

"Which musings confer?" said Father Timothy.

"Of death. I think I have committed homicidal against my most beloved. What an abhorrence I have committed." said Lux.

"What have you to do now?" said Father Timothy. "I will give you absolution after you serve your sentence."

"I must ratiocinate to myself the exact events in rewind that happened the day of the crime. I don't doubt I have committed. I think I am a convict. I dispatched right away to have time to reflect in rustication. But I will return and I know they will find me. Wian will find me."

He has to ratiocinate without denying and confers matters of lucidity. His exodus that entire nocturnal is to be intangible to the pernicious/*dangerous* system. Hallucination usurped him. Alexander manipulated him and matters are disarrayed.

"Who is this Wian? Do you want to rid Wian? If he is not in the way all the attention would be yours. You know Wian is jealous if you have all the attention as well. He is a cynosure-crave monster. Just rid him and there will be no annoyances."

"What about Alice? She would be mad if I touched him. Arghhh…That Wian thinks he is everything walking in and out of Debonair. He sees nobody when I work arduously."

"I sensed your diligence, how can Wian think you're sinecure? He is just trying to pick on you with his orders and astringency. I do not side with Wian. I have confidence in you and you operate that place if you want. Do whatever you want. You are exceptional," Alexander flattered. "Not Wian." He shook his head.

Now he is imprisoned and incarcerated. It is omnipotent that he would be in conquest/*defeat*; in which the only victim is his sister. What pabulum that he had been tricked by Alexander. Sometimes flattery does all the trick.

*   *   *

Back to the lepidoptera story.

There is cri de coeur to the cohesion when he is with iron-willed to rid it a lepidoptera has flown by and infiltrated its scale dust onto his fingers. He does not want to leave dust on his hand and catch the contagion that may be infectant to his health. He once told Alice of the lepidoptera story that is really a moth and how he have to rid the lepidoptera now because it has done thinking and its time is no longer. It has made a mistake and its thoughts are subtraction that it must be rid. It is dimmet.

Moths are attracted to light from the projectile and the cell has the auric field of simulacrum/*replaces reality with its representation* beam. The lepidoptera is projected as such he has to rid the cohesion. He hated cohesion against himself and he would never withstand the pain. It made a sound and the sound would increase rapidly and intensely which would further disorganize and cause disturbances. It has been projected and conjured from somewhere he has made sure there are no kinematics/*motions* of objects returning to his study at the lamp when his imagination leered at a giant monster.

This is all fictitious as though there were monsters that forsooth exist like the requiem/*mass of a death* of a dream. There are personalities of the moth in perspective and moth people of various heights. They are aspired to hinder his pensive having to destruct diurnally when they are the creature of the nocturnal. Hallucination is not letting this down, they are awe-inspiring to destroy their enemies the moth people.

He has sensed the spirit concurrently and there are vituperation/*bitter and abusive language* through the walls. He experiences it nonstop and nonsense verbigeration. His hallucination ensures that civilization is reduced to dross in persiflage/*banter*/*mocking*. He has decided some nighttime to stay at the stationary, the utmost precaution that he would not be banter by the hallucination. It is in the silence of dimmet when the lamp is lighted and then he feels nauseous and suffocates from the insulation.

Alice makes him happy whenever she is there. "You never have to be hurt. It has been my fault. Are you alright? Do you remember the lepidoptera story, Alice? It is a musing of my sentience/*emotions* and conscience," said Lux.

"I think you had told it to me. Is it really a moth or a lepidoptera? asked Alice.

"I think the one that I like most is the moth. Like our mother. There is moth in mother. You resembled her much when she was living."

"I obliged. It is my duty to be mother-like to you."

The lepidoptera would live only if there is light. He has found methods to destroy Ogre this evil spirits monster. He has decided to live and his decision amidst constant scurrility/*hurrying up*. Something alike, he is sensing dissimilitude. It is something alike the lepidoptera or the embodiment/*representation* of something of power compared to the subject. There is no incontinent for he is satori/*enlightenment*. He looks to the time when the next dawn is here during the hour of obscurity. He abhorred the hour of nocturnal in which he would spend in baffled and lethargy. He would revamp himself.

He invented the story of the moths. Moths are not like butterfly. What is the story of the moth? The moth has numerous symbolisms that are portrayed via the plot. It is a terse lepidoptera story Lux thought up and recounted to his sister. In this case it eats the proteinaceous fiber from wool and silk over time transforms into a moth. There is illumination when he is in supplication. The story of the moth is unusual because it does not involve the *transfer* of blood unlike other entomology that might affect the visceral. When he is free from the compunction of his conscience he is the wings of Jupiter forever free from commination/*vengeance* to acknowledge that he lived a healthy and happy life. Illumination has strengthened him to defeat all enemies and philistine.

Somehow here the lepidoptera would tell us its secrets and is buried not spoken of. At time of quiescence the moth combat would be revile and stuck. Then somehow the moth appeared immeasurable. He is reading over the yellow lantern when something query interjected and suddenly caused the vibe to be harrowing. Suddenly a moth hovered over the light causing its shadow to illuminate and magnify onto the shade. It is instinctual and he felt something eerie and immense. The danger is combating and he has not known what to act.

The lepidoptera flew rapidly over head and anchor to overpower the flesh. The 6 feet Lepidoptera keeps anchoring with its urticated abdomen. There is cri de coeur and the crepuscules/*twilight* persisted with the damn vernacular/*language* that would not dissipate, the hallucination. It is huge and it tries to suck the blood from the flesh and sprinkle its scale dusts into to somatic. It tries hard to use its proboscis to inject chemicals into the visceral of the flesh. This has to be done rapidly and rapidly or pabulum. The shadow of the lepidoptera would not diminish and there is continuation of its proboscis sucking on the somatic the duration of night. The cri de coeur/*outcry* would persist and caused him to cry the whole night. He precludes/*makes impossible* the night to be placid and calming, he has to rid the shadow by poisoning it.

We are to deploy a plan to kill the lepidoptera.

Some meaning and legend, the lepidoptera would be destructed at a scene. Trouble has arrived, he can see it afar and this time there is a chronology of past events. We can ensure that the lepidoptera cannot hinder us. Infected it with poison when it anchors to the human's skin with its urticated side. The sounds would not stop infiltration and penetration. He has a preference for solitude; he wanted the sounds to be unsolicited. Somewhere in the circumpolar/*earth's pole* he hears the echoes resound when the hours of the night approached when he converted the psyche of the inmates into righteous and condemned the insane. There are spirits that he revered and spirits that are antagonizing. Out in yonder, perhaps the normal moths are somewhere out there in the winsome/*attractive* lights.

*   *   *

He is afar in a distance at Alcatraz prison, the lepidoptera has to be incarcerated. The shadow is incarcerated and the evil spirits are diminished. Lux finds himself at peace. He awakened in a spasm. There is suspension since he has been on this Earth. After returning from internal cohesion the entire night he has felt himself impossible of sleep. It is noisome/*unpleasant* and he forgot how he could have fallen asleep. Though he remembers he has slept somehow amidst sedulousness/*diligence*. There are rethought from the last and he remembered nothing concrete as though empty when he returned.

There are multiple perspectives of moths and since it is in the order of the lepidoptera has taken heed of this emblem on the side. The past momentous has been a blur and evasive. As though the dream is installation from devices he has not known which kept him up. He would return to the landscape of imagination or if he has thought from his subconscious in time when there are clairvoyant/*six sense* and astronomical/*circumpolar*. Back at civilization, somewhere echoes the cell of the lepidoptera. He destroyed himself when he killed that lepidoptera, there is machination of character. He dies along with Alice, but at least he gets to live in the cell for now.

His mind has been spindled however sobriety/*intelligence*. After the inanition/*tiredness* from nocturnal he has corralled/*gathered* it. It has all been musings and the mind can alter that there is no truth and that truism is evasive. He has turned to his confidence and not aleatory, he has an exodus to make away from the land of lost where he would disclose the musings in runic. It is dangerous from hallucination that can be protracted by infiltrating his thoughts however its vicarious/*through* property is damaged. It would get to the musings then would be lost. He has been strong and let himself to rheumy/*teary eyes*. He knows justifications. He has told it to Alice and knows the way. Perhaps this would buy him some time before the police would pulverize him. He has dispatched on extenuating circumstances. He has to leave in sadness if the musings have been credence. There has been musings and speculation himself how matters adjuncts what he committed to Alice. There is no time for the ultimate adieux to Alice. The musings: Has he hurted Alice? He does not know if Alice is living. He cannot forgive himself.

He has come to see Ratiocination at his lodging. There is secret to death that he keeps to himself that is supreme. Man when they are through must go somewhere ethereal. This is all not reality and they go somewhere etherealized. He is reverent of death and thinks it enlightenment.

The auric field of the night is swift and the night passed by and somewhere the circumpolar are heard the sounds of enigmatic. He has been living in shadows and sciamachy. He would reverse to concern the musing after he is through ratiocination.

Mankind is amaranthine/*unfading*. When we die we leave behind all objects behind us. All things are left behind in the mortal life and we transit onto the afterlife. Do we go on from here, he imagined. Where do our spirits go and some spirits roam and they linger the pain that is on Earth. They linger because their souls become bad spirits and not dissolved.

There is always something mysterious about the cemetery to animate, Lux endorsed it.

Eventually anathema/*hate* has all been forgotten and we enter the kingdom of God.

*   *   *

In the land of the tenebrous/*dark* graveyard where it lay barren the ground serves its purpose for interment. After all, what is this Earth when it decomposes into nothingness, but the stench of miasma in the vast land. When we run out of it, do we inter ourselves on top of one another? Is the ground noisome and filth that it lays the desolation of mankind in bad spirits? We are once in the battlefield of battalion and war.

"The soul of the creature in us is of vast depth. When we fathomed the inquiry of morality, the human's soul has been corrupted. We are hurt by noisome/*unpleasantness*. *What is the value of the human's soul?"* said Ratiocination.

Lux interpolated.

"How long can it withstand human's denigration/*belittle* and injustices do the soul subtract its senses and subdue to corruption? That is what happened to you Lux," said Ratiocination.
" I shall not be subdued," said Lux.

"What have you done to Alice and why have you done it? There is bitter and chthonic/*hellish* all over you. Your air in the field is depraved and there is fume. You have to decontaminate." said Ratiocination.

Lux has relegated/*lowered* to death and not want to discuss sin insofar he reflects and abdicates/*renounce one's throne*. He let Ratiocination palpable of his dithering.

When the conversation of death occurs there is the usual mourning. Its mysticism is beyond graspable and when the topic arises it brings about sentience of eeriness. Usually death is unfathomable.

"Although we know that it is absolution, there is no actual evidence or any recount of life after death or exactly what happens after death. It lies in the realm of mysticism. *Life is portrayed as positive compared to its negativity*," said Lux.

It burns the small ardor of light that illuminates the shadow of the cemetery. There are rows of gravestones that are engraved with epitaphs. Each expresses its memorial before the internment of the dead. Lux read through it while waiting on Alice's. Death awaits the individual at the black gate then they enter perdition or purgatory. There is a new death that occurs every day. Its body is transited into the morgue and processed there for a few days and then it is transited into the cemetery space and interred. The resting place of the corpses at the morgue is elegiac/*mourning*. Before that there is the requiem of the soul.

"The beginning of Earth starts as a phenomenon, one in which is astounding with a battalion/*troop*. When will the creatures on Earth settle the disquietude and learn temperament? It started many years ago in ancient civilization and after revolution have now regenerated in mankind. Though the Earth has transit from its primordial into the temporal there is still hitherto savage. The creatures on Earth have arisen from the organic substances or whatever means.

Violence does not end violence and how much will the generation continue? How much carnage does it resolve to every life there is a resolution and death awaits us. When death strikes, portends of time that life will end they will leave the temporary life behind and transgress to the next. Do we have recollection of the setting for none have been to the end of Earth before, to see if it exists and what happens life after death. Death, when it arrives, is the end of the mortal life and where will we journey or is it just a terminal that ends in ashes and desolation. There are the remnants of their spirits that speaks of tenement," said Ratiocination.

Lux has thought of death. There is a full-moon tonight. It is a chilly night. By the time the visitors evacuated from the cemetery the luminescence of the moon was out. The black gate is closed. The morgue is kept with elegiac music that keeps the spirit of the corpses asleep. Some nights the spirits awakened and it would roam on Earth. Lux talked to himself while he dressed himself in his cassock.

There are nights when the spirits are disquieting. The crepuscular weather would be ominous and foreshadows danger. The cemetery vibe is moribund and elegiac. This time of the year there are dews on the gravestone that makes the stone wet and changes the color of its stone a darker gray. The cemetery gate is opened by 8 o'clock in the microcosm/*universe*. It welcomes visitors to the first interment ceremony that is when they remove the corpses from the mortuary into the vehicle/hearse that drives it down into the mile-long road of the cemetery stationed for the purpose of interment.

"Sometimes the spirit of the moth comes back to tell us that there is light. That you should look onward than the sacrilegious/*blasphemous* situation, where it will be exasperated to perceive light and wisdom. One event after another of peak and fall it is ceaseless nonstop and amain/*at full* speed and we must go on from here to see the paragon/*the perfect example*. We are suffering noisome. Somewhere the paean/*song of praise* resounds over the hill that sprawls everlasting and we can do peace, there will be peace of the soul, quiet alas," said Ratiocination.

In returning to unfathomable/*unthought* he would regain the musings. He has remonstrated/*complained* through Ratiocination. The tears that are falling are from the knowledge he collates and the memories of it caused him to retract and somehow the pain can be released from the lacrimal glands.

Sad Damian, the Assassin

"Killing is never right and justified, says the
law."

"Everybody gets only one chance at
anything worth doing, only the first."

I remember nothing. I can recall nothing. It was
all killing. Somehow they brainwashed me to work for
them, but I remembered nothing else. Nothing before
that nothing happened. It was nasty and harrowing
how I drowned and suffocated. I was gasping for
breath when inundated with water in my nostril. I was
searching and prehensile for anchorage and nothing. I
do not swim. Then there was a black out and here I
am. With my recruiter and I knew nobody else. What
do I know?

It is never right to kill. But some people
deserve it and that is my commission. My tasks to rid
these people who do not deserve their lives and they do
not get to live. Because they had done something bad.
We had given them time, it was too late. This time it
was too late. But time can be ad libitum if you are going
nowhere and uneven. Sometimes I feel like this as
well. As though I am getting nowhere. And only if all
the bad guys are riddance, do life be lived with
meaning. But there are flashbacks somewhere else.
Somewhere immemorial. And silence immemorial. I
cannot recall it and have nothing to say of it.

Am I a killer? A borned killer? A natural killer? What would they judge me?

Am I a psychopath? I don't think I am because it is very pathological to rid those most vilest beings on earth that I do not pronounce humans and can. They are breeds of animals. I work like a machine and I listen to orders. When I get an order to do my task I would not go about prowling and get right to it. That is why I became the top assassin quickly in little time. Weapons of target are usually a noose, a hatchet or a carbine from afar used by a marksman. I tell you I seemed dangerous but I am actually the protector of humanity. These bad guys deserve death.

When I execute I don't hesitate because it would render me weak but it is a nasty job. When I get done there is euphoria out of it when the aim is down. When the target is killed then my night is finished. There are sighs of relief that the bad guys can no longer do harm. That I have done good deeds to eradicate them forever.

I like the night. I am Damian. My ID says Damian Florence. I think I still need to explain gradually and piecemeal. One at a time I will explicate? How do I know? Is it genetics? Is it innate and inherent in human beings to know right from wrong. But of course killing is wrong-doing. There is no killing. I am passionate about these bastards I kill at night. I get the thrill of it because they are so caustic and biting in my head. They are dumbfounded losers.

There is a piece in me that is heartfelt. There is a girl named Amy. Amy Tanner. Amy is an accessory. I don't know if this person is relevant to my life or will permanently be around. That is why I think she is an accessory. My life, in contemporary times, is not steady. Somehow I don't think anything in the present really is my life and that there is a different life before all of this. Maybe I don't like what I do. Do I really like being an assassin? I am neutral. I am apathetic. Sometimes it conflicts with who I am because it gets to me, my compunction because no matter what there is this yucky icky business about killing that nobody wants and likes. But I have to deal with the tasks because that is my job. My commission. To protect the innocent.

Can you believe there are that many bad people in the world? There are just as many bad people in the world as there are good. But I believe there are more good. The world is a good place. Man, there are so many people in the world. That is why there are that many bad people. That many targets to rid if they do not live right.

I can't read Amy and she can't read me. But we have a connection that when I kiss her there are flashbacks of someone else. Images of someone else appear. It seems like my old self returns and memories of the past are elicited. I keep finding clips of the past whenever we touch and I want to discover more of this feeling. I don't exactly like kissing Amy, but there is a double self to me that likes that person behind there that I kissed. Maybe in the past. Before, a long time ago if this past makes up part of the present. Or it is just kissing someone that makes me remember something in the past. But I wasn't exactly kissing Amy but someone else. I think there is another name to her.

It kept echoing Charmaine. Who is this Charmaine? I haven't told Amy. I think I am going to tell Amy. I don't think I am in love with her, what is love anyway, but there is someone else. Or images of someone else keeps appearing and I would keep being distracted, like I'm not supposed to and cause disappointment.

What is love anyway? I have never been in love or have I been in a relationship before with a girl named Charmaine. That is why I keep conjuring her when Amy and I kissed? Am I supposed to have a second love? Or is it just one? I am in oblivion. Before they brainwashed me? I never inquire. When I think of Charmaine I think of why I am doing what I am doing and tied down to them as an assassin.

Alexander Tanner is Amy's father who trains assassins. He saved my life one time when I drowned off the cliff. Did he save my life or did he sabotage it by making me an assassin? He said I am the stronger force. We want to create the strongest army to rid them all. To rid off all the people that do not deserve life. My targets are the bad guys. Those who are futile and should cease to exist. They no longer have a purpose in life and need to be rid. Usually it is not by their will but we want them exterminated for a better earth.

But is killing ethical? We can leave it to the bidding law but capital punishment is abolished.

One night I was out using a noose relentless because this man raped and his child twice. And he is free to be outside the jurisdiction. They haven't arrested him and don't plan on it because it is their father and no one called 911 on the brutish dad. Who cares, kill him, why live anyway. But the ultimate law of the land is no killing allowed and even the ten commandments. This cannot be subjective. To me, the brutish dad deserves death. Everybody gets one chance; you bastard. Only the first.

I think I lost my memories or they brainwashed me to my life the way it is now? But how was it before? There are times I wonder but my mind would be blank.

Where do I find this Charmaine? What does she have to do with me? I think we are a pair already before Amy came along. But to be fair I don't know. That is my thought. Let's get all of this straight. I don't know how to love. Not the kind that is carnal romantic love anyway. Where is my family? I have been searching and pondering on this. Don't we all have families that are our special destiny? One in which we cannot escape other than being an assassin. Is that right? There is discipline, seeing what is right. Where is mine? Am I doing what is right? Then my mind would go blank.

KISMET

"IT IS AN ISOMORPHISM THAT WE ARE TOGETHER."

"ALICE IS ICONIC."

Out on a vessel one day Alice and Wian were celebrating their 30th anniversary and enjoying the breezes by the sea. Wian just purchased a yacht and takes Alice out to relish the sea to have some inspirations for her paintings as well.

"I can't believe we are together and married. Many people nowadays celibate and not marry. Our marriage is a holy marriage. That is why it is possible that it transpired. How many years is it upcoming?" pondered Alice.

"I think sweetheart it will be close to 30 years." said Wian

"That is coral."

"That is beautiful."

"Do you remember how we met?"

"We met at the library one day when we were young and used to go to the library all the time to study. I would run into you all the time and you were quite a charm to look at. You're beautiful Alice."

Alice laughed. "Thanks Wian. You're always

saying that all the time. It's not like I'm an actress. But it's sweet I guess."

Alice laughed again out loud at Wian's consideration. He looked confused and then it seemed to Alice that she made him think about his frequent praises. So she laughed.

Alice is always laughing and Wian enjoys her laugh timeless.

Out on the sea, Alice saw a dolphin jump out of the water and does a flip and then back into the water.

"Look over there, there is a dolphin."

"I like the cruise, we always see sea animals in the water. I saw one earlier. Just didn't mention it because we always see it."

Wian is not a lover of animals compared to Alice. Alice loves animals, especially aquatic animals. They talked, quipped, and kissed.

Later when they were sunbathing on the vessel Wian put her hair up in a coiffure and they discussed their girl's twin and the adopted son while Alice painted the sky and horizon on top of the sea and dolphins.

"Do you like, Einstein with Adam? Those two are adorable together to me. They are always together like best friends. Like us almost, they say best friends have to see each other every day and it is fine to see normal friends only once a week. I think they see each other every day at the hospital."

"You are always right honey. What a good match. Einstein and Adam. I wasn't conative of that. The meaning of conative is emotion cognitive."

"I already knew."

"Are you lying?" He looked suspicious at her, but in a pernicious quipping way.

"I never lie. Why would I lie? " questioned Alice.

"I am more a man of my words than you." replied Wian.

"I don't think so, it is me too." answered Alice.

"Words are power, I would never lie either. I am glad that of you Alice, but I think we will forget."

"Do you think I lie?" said Alice.

"I don't think you lie." said Wian.

"That's good." Alice agreed.

"It is Adam's last year in training as a resident of psychiatry and he will make a great mate to our Einstein."

"Do you think it's weird that they marry though because…" pondered Alice.

"He's adopted…Well it's a separate germline. It would be isomorphism compared to homology."

"And what is that exactly?"

"It is the same traits from different ancestry compared to a common ancestry.

"I told you if I don't know, I will tell," demanded Alice

"I am straightforward like that too," agreed Wian.

"So that's fine, Einstein and Adam," said Alice.

"I wish them many children just like us," said Wian.

"I think Adam will ask for her hand or do you think we should just assign and matchmake them?" asked Alice.

"It should be matchmade. That couple is starcrossed. I agreed. Like us." said Wian.

Alice is a small pretty girl in her 50s. She is always two digits in weight compared to the other smaller girls who are eighty pounds. Alice used to be in the mid-eighties but after gestation she remained in the nineties, but her hair cut in a bob pixie. When she gets back to eighty-five pounds she grows her hair out. Alice is approximately 5 feet and one inch. Maintaining her weight is her way of keeping herself healthy, happy, and successful. Starving is her poignant luxury.

Wian is 6 feet one inch and keeps his weight undeclared.

Alice's twin girls are most beautiful as well. Both girls are iota below 5 feet and small and petite. Their feet are both size 2 same as Alice. What if Cinderella had twins? Cinderella are both the twin girls. Einstein and Charmaine. Charmaine would never marry but have beaus. Alice and Wian leave it up to Charmaine but she wants to be like Grandpa and preserved. So she does not want to marry and keep herself virgin. That leaves Einstein the obligation to wed and continue the ancestral tree if she wants. Einstein and Adam are supple and do not mind anything.

Our beaus are the sentinels at the hospital, the Florence and the Collins. They are treasured and invaluable young men to the Wian. Both have shown affection to Charmaine. We selected the Florence to be with us and so does Charmaine and maybe when time permits they will consolidate.

Damian Florence and Charmaine Brown Girffit's romance story started out with a kiss. He was amnesiac because of past history and one time Damian mistaken another different kiss for Charmaine when he was amnesiac and he felt queer about it and somehow traced this true love for Charmaine when he gradually and piecemeal recollected his former memories. Damian is a trained assassin who had lost his memories. He hates everything about his assassinating life. When his memory was lost he met another girl called Amy. They kissed and somehow his memory came back because he remembered a different first kiss with Charmaine.

Charmaine wants to remain single and celibate and remain pageant and virgin. Though the two never kiss again after she does not feel the same and are platonic/*friends*. Charmaine cannot accept Damian. She cannot love a murderer.

CITIES OF THE SEA

"DAMN LUX, HE KILLED BOTH OUR LOVED ONE. SO
DO THE RIGHT DEED, FOR THE WRONG REASON."

Wian is a builder. He has the potential to build the universe. Has the masons finished building at this time? Wian sees the masons insulating, cutting and sawing, glazing the glass to construct the architectural building in high rise. At sunrise there is sun ray sprawling against the vitreous where the masons are glazing transmitting the intensity of the sun to the glass. They are still up there on the machines and equipment of hoisting power constructing levels above the ground, feeling the light wind. They have engineered from blueprints to make the construction precise. He can tarry up where the derrick is with hoist power and the masons go on to perform their tasks.

Inside the compartment there rests the lives of hundreds of inpatients. It is warm on the inside and normally because it is by the sea the temperature can drop outside. Debonair is a refuge, a place of safety, salvation and warmth.

Once upon a time, Alice would take her canvas out on the dunes and paint various pictures of the cities against the sea background. We have Wian and he will protect us till the end. How gargantuan is the vast ocean and body of water and where does it end on the other side but the globe a circle and where are beginnings in a circle. Wian will take Alice to the end of the world and again. Alice smiled to herself of her sweet husband. There is nobody as much as Wian on this whole earth and he is mine and mind. I am the luckiest person on earth. They are alone together as well as together in presence.

"I know exactly what you are thinking Wian," Alice said to herself laughing and pirouette and evanescent in front of Wian. Wian was thinking while walking up the dunes next to the two twin girls of past timing and misses Alice's presence.

Alice is a charm. She is always happy and cheerful. Never eating and she would always say, "I am starving and that is my poignant luxury." Wian memorized it too. Alice is always anorexic and she was happy to be underweight. Alice's image in a pink dress twirling around on the dunes is captivating to Wian. He was down and misses Alice when they would walk as family across the sand bank since the girls were young. Now they are coming of age, and next to Wian are the two girls only. Both are similar to Alice's remains. But they can never compare to Alice in his heart. Alice always tries and wins.

Both Einstein and Charmaine were in tears.

"She was our best friend," said Einstein.

"How can I ever repay mom?" said Charmaine. "She gave us everything. She'd given us the world."

"Our life is on fire with mom, now it's like the ember and excelsior have extinguished in our fireplace. Everything around the house is cold," said Einstein.

"How can we ever replace mom? I always want to grow up to be exactly like mom," said Charmaine.

"How can I do that to you two? Don't fret, there is me and I will make it up to you just like your mom. I am both dad and mom from now on. You two are still so young to be without both parents. You never have to feel alone when mom is not here. You know I am here. I will try to take mom's place as well," said Wian.

"We know you are a great dad and mom..." they both said and both started to tear up in solaces of mom's presence.

"Have you thought of Damian, Charmaine? "

"He is nowhere to be found. Before uncle Lux raided the hospital. I already noticed Damian missing," said Charmaine.

"Do you want to find him? I might know where he is to be found. But expect surprises."

"Where is he?"

"I think he is with Lux." Both were appalled because uncle Lux is a criminal on the news.

"Damian has become the top shooter, top assassin for Alexander. He had something to do with Lux too. I hear Alexander detests anybody better than him and tantalizes and pressured Lux. Had Lux listened to me he would be on the bright side. But Lux is defying that is why he might join the dark side with Alexander. I am not sure who this Alexander is, but I'm not sure if Alexander knows me how I got this information. That is why all the trouble must have started for Lux. Lux is not discrete and pretends and can't tell good from evil. That man is very dark and manipulative, stay away from him. He must have manipulated Lux into trying to kill dad and that was when mom intercepted to protect me. He got Lux on the bad side when his will was dithering."

"What happened to Damian? Is he out of his mind? What freak, an assassin? He's worse than Uncle Lux. I don't see that in Damian," said Charmaine. "What did he do to Damian. What is Damian doing with such a dark man? Damian is day."

"I think something is wrong with Damian and we are about to find out why. Let's come find him in the city with Alexander. He purportedly thought it to me. I think he might be brainwashed. Don't be surprised if he doesn't remember you."

"OMG. How impossible," said Charmaine admonished.

"By the way, just because Lux has done it to his loved one, there is more reason to care and pay for it. More reasons to atone for a good person. Because Alice acquitted him, there is more reason to redeem, That makes Lux that much dumber. I don't know the case of Damian yet. The law abides that there be no capital punishment. I think he is not the culprit, there is someone behind all this manipulation. Dumb. Right now I hate Lux most. What an ass."

"I hope Damian is on the right side," said Charmaine.

"Lux is more pernicious and conniving. Damian is still young and was brainwashed. Lux knows. Not Damian," said Wian. "I know it is only because of Alice that will get to him. His conscience will do it. Your mother is innocent. He will be that to her."

LEPIDOPTERA TWO

"LUX CONTINUES TO TALK TO HIS CONSCIENCE AS HE
ENTERS THE ZONE OF REPENTANCE IN THE SUMMIT OF THE
MOUNTAINS."

"HE BEGINS TO BE CONSCIENTIOUS AS TO WHAT THE
LEPIDOPTERAS ARE TELLING HIM."

One time he had lepidoptera dust and snow
melted them. It had been emblematic. The lepidoptera
has many symbolisms as can be interpreted from the
maxim of the lepidoptera story. In either maxim like
Gestalt psychology there is either side to light. The
lepidoptera has a natural proclivity or conative/*emotional
cognitive* for light and symbolism of Lux
sciamachy/*shadow*.

In another symbolism the lepidoptera is an
attraction to light. The lepidoptera instinctively
attempts to correct by turning toward the light. There
is the chimerical of the lepidoptera that anchors over
the body an instance right before the sarcophagus is
close to being interred. Revelation has occurred and the
police investigation is protracted and the lepidoptera has
been the path to the discovery of the killer. This has all
been musing and self-evident. It does not concern the
business that its other phylum the butterfly tells its
lesson. It is effervescent/*lively*. It is about deftest, writ,
and right how the good man's thoughts can be
corrupted on its own by puzzling deprecation
manipulations to see oneself in shadow and
self-abnegation. The man is to be trial for his integrity
and character. The hallucinations have taken character

from him without realizing that is how he has become vicious. He never likes to speak of this. He is caring about time spuriously, the sequences of events in which had taken place. When the world is an implacable/relentless place, he acquires for himself the attitude so that life is lived in cadence and tranquility. Though, it is a place of decadence and amidst its chaos one must maintain righteousness and silence.

The world is governed by a foundation of morality. Is it instinct to do right? Is it justified by the mind or the heart? No one knows him in this planet on the gargantuan land map and somewhere he is escaping or exploring for eternally. Over the scenic oasis of the world there is wondrous. There are landscapes that are the greatest test of the psyche. When you see its landscape picture emotions that you could not somehow conjure it to the conscious and self-realization therefore is self-abnegating when arbitrating. Often he finds himself at this stance when he is conscientious.

Then revised himself when he is getting the idea of the 'moth' in the order lepidoptera. One night when a lepidoptera has landed in transverse orientation on the shade of a lamp. In an environment and atmosphere in which he has been listless and lethargic from the day's expenditure and by vesper crepuscules into night he is at work arduously once more to get ends meet.

Its visage is bloodless he warns, it does not involve the *transfer* of blood. On account of touch and sensate it would leave scale dust onto the skin of another individual. He discovers if the moth is actual bloodless or it is the recipient that it must protects itself anent/*about*. He discovers if anything implacable is done by will or by foist/*force*? Lux has supplicated for illumination however corruption and oppressive has altered the state of his deportment. We question the meaning of human's existence, why evil must be perpetrated and why we can not all collide. This is naive thinking of neoteny, have he compiled evil only to accumulate of violence and hatred.

He deployed the musing when it is safe, not to be subdued by negative influence. He dozed into a siesta and he is breathing to control his thoughts that have been unconsciously, uncontrolled in which he brought to quiescence. When he awoke he was in unfamiliar terrain surrounded by scenic nature. He is now able to take a deep breath and relieve himself from the axis of tension that has occurred over nocturnal. It has been horrendous and unnerving and if he thought about the obfuscation/*unclear* would give a migraine. Days after days of effacing the oppression in the fracas/*commotion* he can depict solecism/*blunder* and depletion of his conscience once he has brought it to self-realization. Will his character ever be the same when the stream of conscience is calling out?

Sciamachy is a shadow whose despair is subtended by a moth. In which his imagination has sought to kill. The moth is however too rapid on its wings and has escaped. The moth has been a disturbance and caused his allergen. Over routine, appearance of the moth has caused him to become irritated and his trauma due to pain lacerated and driven him to the profundity of a sociopath Lepidoptera killer. This is Lux.

Phenomenon exists. It does not happen because of coincidence; he thinks they are signs of God. Its existence is fictitious and then momentarily as though it has appeared out of thin air a moth flew subtending across midair and landed on the window. It's exegetic/*explanation* intricate. How does he come about to the idea of a moth primarily? Is he adept at the faculty? He is able to sense life; a different being.

We are not capable of its demise. Its utterance of death...The moment he spoke of its last dialogic imagination the animal flew across and landed on the window. It was not there before. How could it have been through? Momentously the animal flew away when it was left unattended and then it went into the demiurgic/*universe.*

When he was young, he used to think that lepidoptera germinated from the yellow lantern light. It may have just laid its eggs there and hatched into the avian sect.

The moth lay there shriveled under the yellow lantern. Its flies flap in repetitive motion a few seconds before the reader snaps it with pressure making sure of its demise. Seldom there would be a moth that gets stuck in the lamp. It's frizz would cause and provoke the reader into obnoxiousness. Minutes later it would not stop its nuisances. It is time to kill.

The energy would be dispensed into killing the insect. Moths are a type of insects that are the initial conception then later he thought it over. Insects are not allowed to fly the axiom/*accepted truth* of life and nature.

Moths are Lepidoptera.

Its motion compulsive and convulsive before there is infernal. It lay there hurt, no longer capable of its fly. It is about to be rid of because there are no means for this existence.

Within seconds after, it is dead. Its corporeal and the rind of its wing pressured into segments. Its guts exploded from its envelope. The moth powder is scattered on the plane, there is no chance of its survival, left for infernal.

Under the magnifying glass there is its segmentation. The moth lay shriveled on the table platform and its residue of salt powder forms the white residue on the platform of the woods.

.

He watched crepuscules transcend and cessate into the night. We get beat out by the irritation and events that verve at the margent when its deadline has met. It has been passé and terminal but its existentialism has not yet exterminated thereby causing irate. It has been incessant and interminable. The spirits are bollocks/*nonsense* and disorganized causing his vigor to lacerate and become fatigue. During nocturnal he has been disturbed and frightened by the spirit that has appearances of intimidating forms. It has been recurring and he is trapped in its system. It has been sometime now that it has been causing him query feelings. Mind and experience are contravention and somehow he believed he is able to conjure the lepidoptera. He might lose vigor as the shadows of the opaque is overcasted and outside in the shadow of the dark are the shadows of dim. This time when he say shadow and the intonation resounded, there was something pounding on his stomach. It is inundated with query and eldritch/*dark*. When he stopped the cantillation/*chanting* the disquietude stopped. He must be seeing a spectre of sciamachy, the enemy shadow of himself in the motion of inanition/*tiredness*.

Outside in the frigorific aria are feral pigeons scattered on the gravel road gathered on either side of the street. It is eternal schadenfreude/*laugh at someone's suffering* and viscosity; abduction of the conscience and corruption. Their soul has rested somewhere in the graves on the barren ground where it lay interred beneath the layers of Earth's ground and the other hapless/*unfortunate* creatures are perhaps paying in reliving another form of dross. This squalid form is often considered a pest or even vermin, owing to concerns that they spread diseases. It nibbles the sediments and debris on the road for survival in the city, times they conflict with people when its population becomes irate. They try to rid the reduced form of the creature before the afterlife that has reincarnated into the reduced form. There scatter on the gravel ground on the street side of the city these flocks of columbidae. He watches the light outside amidst the Neolithic street then the shadow is dismissed and the auric field is no longer explosive of unsettling spirits. They are divagating spirits that have needed to pass on to the next life and not roam the streets to pollute the aria with a pestilential atmosphere. Whenever he has thought of the spirits, it seems to be conjured and it runs the shivers down his torso. He gets frigorific perhaps, the spirits can move on to another life and be reincarnated.

For some time, he has not wanted to remember the spirits (he has commanded it to dismiss and to be with someone else) then, at times, they have sought to connect with his soul. When night he has thoughts of the events of the conjuration of the spirit it iterated/*uttered*, once more tried to connect. It frightened him that the thoughts were incomprehensible.

At morning adret/*slope of the mountain that faces the sun*, the plenum is silent and he can feel the motion from nocturnal. He has researched on the lepidoptera and the idea of the nexus is conjured. The lepidoptera depicts some ideology of lepidoptera people. It happens in a dream when he analyzes the perspectives of the lepidoptera. Other symbols of the Lepidoptera are an attraction to light in darkness, it perfects our inherent psychic abilities, personal power, and happiness.

At parts, he is being imaginative and his imagination is the exigency/*explanation* from the apperception of the spirits. Then the connexion of them terminated him to feel query and irate throughout as he has made connection with the lepidoptera. Somehow when he has thought it out completely there are no details lingering and then when it is stuck inside his head or is evaded. There is something confounding which has manifested power before him.

First he has not believed in superstition or taboo of any lore/*myth* until he is informed by the spirits that actually become animated as a scribe. Words are not words alone; there are thoughts behind them that can give thoughts anima. Actually everything that has effort has some anima to it generated from the energy, life and auric field that is brooded over it. (The moth which is the effector has anima in it that perpetuates.) This anima can be transmitted to cause variant emotions when the text is imbibed. Thoughts even have this form of energy that when parallel with the text emits this photon of energy. He believes an occasion he felt imbibed by the spirits as though they are robbing verve and through some plane he has nexus being paranoid he has sent the spirits away to another being through telepathic stance.

The spirits can be conjured into the world as brute form. There is the barking of the black dog when there is anima of the deceased spirits being conjured. Some nocturnal when the spirits have been conjured the brute has kept barking to entire stupefaction/*unconciousness*. He has no understanding of this but the actual spirits have internal cohesion in brute form where the brute would be caused to reply to the spirits. Brutes can sense spirits and the spirits communicate as brute manifestation. Most spirits are not stuck in the underworld and they move on to the next life if there is a life after death and some spirits are reincarnated. A second, he is the nexus between the underworld and Earth as though the spirits are being conjured. He sees the nature of taboo/*forbidden* in the fear of demons.

Really he does not need much in life but there are mysteries that he has not discovered and by living he is bombarded with the mysticisms of the universe.

He has taken a few verses from David Hume, he fancies himself enveloped with the deepest darkness on every side. He is a skeptical thinker. Is it possible for us to find the true answers to these perplexing questions? Man flings these questions at the face of life and waits and waits but finds no answer till he totters into the grave.

At illumination God invests man with intelligence, a faculty which is fully equal to discovering the truth about his own self and his character. There are the riddles of life which puzzle the sages and busy themselves with these dark enigmas but still mankind gropes for the answers. The exodus has been for this reason and through reflections he made himself cogent/ *clear and convincing.*

Now he has discovered himself and the true meaning of life and he sees himself as faculty to be improved with the sharp ability to perceive people's true nature. He climbs to the summit of the misty mountain to see the acme reveal before him foremost and he has to find them where the land space sprawls out before him and where there is darkness he can see light. He has put himself at the point here he can see from the tallest mountains to see the musing sprawling. Where he has been is eternal darkness and he is not able to see light on the other side in distal and everywhere the zone has been darkened. At the axis of expressive tension, he is able to think the thoughts emanating from what is expressed or the natural common condition until mankind thinks; is able to think and look into his heart to find the character in himself. He believes he is at the summit the entire time. At the summit has given him writ however there is generation of doubts and to abstain from furthering this has made him nervous. He has discovered never to be demeaned by life and never to be exalted by them. There is tendency to act opposite for safety to divert the current of thoughts and eventually there is admixture.

In truth, how does he see the self; as an entity correlating with the same ancestry of the universe through rituals and convention and the way of being. Then an event would happen to alter and transform the being from the working of the rest of the world. Now he idolizes himself no other higher beings because he is betrayed and if ever there are senses of insecurity, he would feel the depths in adrenaline. He has surpassed solecism/*blunder* and the breach cannot abduct or change his character; the formation of the self is solid. Later to all, the adrenaline he finds in himself is effacing the moral force.

There is some form of security and truth that is God when the illumination answered his supplication/*prayer to beg for something in need* amidst the dark Earth. Then he goes to stand at the summit to see the many colors of the extramural and in the layers of the adret he can see the view thereby opening a new pathway to the musings of these thoughts where there are now visionaries. Visionaries have recorded perfectly genuine experiences and now he is able to remember. The musings that he corralled is the stream of mental quiet that has at least carried him beyond the intellect.

He sees every aspect and insights from this summit, let the interchange and disjunction of his soul

82

be healed, protected as he has improved character and bless his deportment. Over the minutes the outskirts from afar are moving closer and prevalent. He is exonerated and himself is given back its vigor no longer under the weight and he is uplifted from the prick of the conscience if he returns and serves his sentence. Alice will forgive him. She had promised. He will be free from guilt because she forgives him.

Somewhere in ethereal, he hears the sounds of the harp played by the cherubim he felt ever so free from oppression. The oppression caused by the allusive/*indirectly* implying self of his beliefs and everything of him that this instance has won triumphant. There is no plectrum of guitar; there is a beacon of light.

This instance is the best moment when he is uplifted and knows the truth. He is free that the greatest certainty in knowledge comes only in the sphere of self.

Certainly, he can change over the years from fracas/*quarrel* and the principles that he has altered in the present has given him revelation; these are the maxim of change. He does not know how he has evolved into the person that he is now, and the mind and experience is together therefore it has been swift. Beliefs are altered from visionaries and they are solidified.

The mind is experience, what he thinks is even greater expanse than his experience because thoughts are imaginative versus his experience is a spectre of the eyes and visionary. In a sense, people can take experience away from you that is sacred but can never contaminate your thinking because it is bricolage/*creation from a diverse range of available things*. Therefore, experience can be changed; the way that he thinks. Experiences are happenstance/*coincidences*; those are also appearances of God in anonymity. Thoughts are intrinsic qualities that no one can replicate.

The demon tries to ruin our experience by infiltrating our thoughts to corrupt it and make us evil by evil thoughts. It is thoughts that perpetrate our actions into experience therefore the mind is sacred. The fool has ruined our morale and tries to abduct our vigor so that our soul is dead. He may find revelation and revamp as he urges to regain every day of his life that the system has verbigeration.

There are pedestrians in the crosswalk and he secerned/*distinguished* the people in motion at en route, it triggers anger and aggression when he discerned that he is trifled. He has passion of being at acme of writing and nighttime he tarried up/*stay up* numerous meditation to work on his efforts. There is reflection of the journey through life in which he has expatiate/*speak or write at length in details*. He is gifted and the inspirational words that aid the suffering through endurance of pain one would never relinquish to the misgivings and forfeit one's soul to alterity. The ulterior forces are bulwark of the internal he has kept it from invading his internal and able to be privy where it is most covert.

It is love that alters their mentality by loving

moiety/*half*, resentment is relieved from temptation to do evil thereby finding love is recovery, hope, and strength. He no longer convinced the world in the stance he sees in a sundry/*several*, paragon/*perfect example* today and his will is to transcend. He does not like infinity without measure as true measures are within and reflect to see the vicious journey of the past.

The sounds dissipate into nature and at the end of the universe somewhere he can still hear its echoes resound. For the voices of the world that are not heard are in damnation vested distal outskirts. Their contamination sprawls to the other side of the Earth and what he can perform is to exterminate it through combat and constant striving of the secrets that he possesses covetous.

This is one voice cri de coeur in the stricken world. However, the impasse/*dead end* they may cause and the damages of their infliction attend to cost. It is a silent world where the voices are not heard but there are thousands of those suffering not being able to reach out their messages to anyone. It is the world of dimension implacable/*unrelenting* is played by the ears and never knows truism. Where has he heard this mental disquietude in which reality is not seen as barricaded from society. He is reaching out but is not heard because society does not survey but only attends to one's own portent. He has been living on his own while there are no senses of community thereby no sameness for the voices heard in the material world one does not give heed but is the exactitude of portent. Nature is a veil in which he only sees the pretension except the privy eyes. The scribe in which he shares his experience of an empty space that is mystic and ethereal; it is never ending tantalizing and reviling.

He has been forgiving and forgetful when memories of yesterday of longiloquence are no longer recollection. He is only evasive that he would not remember the experience and his mind would not be bothersome. In previous years before the formation of consciousness and recognition the events had been a blur. He no longer remembers there are imprinting except that everything has been vaguely similar to the city's lamp. He has not understood except what has been peripheral, not what he interpolated of the massiveness of the burgeoning city. Then when the destruction happened he is lost, today is harder to live and while there is conundrum he is sensing it give off. Then one day he has known better when there is the first account of pain when pain has first infiltrated through the fenestration and into his consciousness and the conscience that he has primal sense inequality that some action must be done. While he is vested in this matter the distal circular orbits or somewhere the universe has heard his echoes but there is no reply. He has not experienced it therefore has no thought of the concept. How can they penetrate the mind and thoughts? The road before him is mystic.

After, he has been subjugated because of alacrity/*readiness* and the need for experiences. The world has fraught him of associative just because he has binary obverse views that nature is of scene and crime. He claims experiences as an advantage or experiences as an obligation to endure. Foremost he urges that it has been an advantage when in the nascent years of naivety, he has been associative than in the later he no longer calls for fame or the heed for experience. For the demiurge no longer has justification other than the act on infinity. He wants to pass by the world for utmost experience not the mundane glide through the eyes of misjudgment. It becomes an experience when he shares it with someone and if he has perception of it all one is heeded and not susceptible or perceptive of another ear.

He has turned another page every day of his living. He would be encouraged differently by experiences. He has been a scribe overnight and done the task penning his suspension. It is situational and our experiences can be havoc before there is fatality. The interchangeable deportment can develop mannerism from musing. He can see vespers at this moment as there is crepuscular twilight declension in darkness leaving shadow on the leaves in darkness no longer visible. Its outline no longer matters than the conglomerate of its shadows.

The volume crescendo causes incantation and irritation that would not subside and no matter what the situation is foisting there is nothing that can alter except to differentiate. He has contended this musing and performed it himself for the sake of his personal power and happiness.

As the passage of the year bygone, every day is lived in perseverance and determination to reach the greatest acme. On an evening, Handle has gone out to the world to see the paragon of the day before it has bygone. It is an act free from consequences however be that he has been at the lodging he would not vision the burgeoning city and its bustle. On the contrary though some nighttime adventure he might find revelation as he has not been there the same and there has been solecism. There could have been travesty/*distorted representation* that would be avoided if he has decided to stay and skip the venture, however if the evening calls for it, it is only piety if there is vocation and taboo where he has to attend in the auric field.

He has chosen recourse from solipsism and ventured an exodus. While the experiences of today are happening he effused an energy to the world in the partake experience. It is mind musing turning into experience in which has been his ephemeral decision. Tonight his decision will be tabulated and the events will be recounted on isomorphism/*similarity in organisms resulting from different ancestry*; he returns.

The clouds tell many stories. If we were able to see it, we should look beyond it to see the best views and natural scenery. It is the way humans work (if there are sinister clouds) we must see depth. This visionary is of clouds if there is pessimistic resultant. That day over the summit he has not remembered again. He has not seen clouds or has not remembered. A picture is a capture of truism. Do you think it has all been hope? There is hope. He remembers the hour standing at the summit and certainly there have been no clouds like the silver boulder reaching to the sky. Hope can be further and expand into veridic experiences. The truth he sees is like a vesture, we must find out the hidden.

In another sense, the exodus is along the journey to covetous, privacy, and hope in which many he has forsaken as chance when time has not been right. Perhaps our soul has been searching another venue, but some parts of it still remain. We cannot let the pestilential atmosphere brood over us and then we will be intercepted, the self and humanity will be lost.

Censure, thereby in we should never watch the clouds for the eyes are deceptive if it does not open to see the views of a window that is slightly ajar and let light stream in. This pertains to every one of us and not let them devour our soul. Let us not be infiltrated by deprecation and pestilence to give up the stream of conscience. He writes this to tell for any querent that might be seeking knowledge to the Secret Pathway that has been barricaded for fear of the demons; for hope of fear to not be scattered and dejected. He is prone to seek darkness in the depth of ethereal light.

Originally he has the idea of the lepidoptera and then over research and imagination it has diverged into in depth to delve into the stream of conscience.

Are there no striving in life? At every point in life he has been battling against unrighteousness and the stream of our conscience. He is constantly fighting his plight against the current of the diurnal tides. Every crepuscule war is expected, where he must rid it for peace to be restored from the evil of the planet. They try to obstruct us from senses and reasons there is cri de coeur...

The events have been historic, never minding the past; it is time for innovation and time to progress. If he look forward to see the visionary ahead of him there are millions years of existence and today is of a unit; a light year that will pass and will not be remember unless he has amanuensis/*remembrance* of its recording the pandemonium/*chaos* that is happening on this Earth. Where will he go on from here after the last light year occurrences to fathom beyond enigma? There has been the ajar window that resounds the stream of consciousness when humans are not destructed what is left of the world in the future a thousand or millions years from now, will he cease to exist or has he lived a similar life before existentialism. There is a recording of every phenomenon that occurs on Earth. What is more, he does not know what will happen to Earth and its inhabitants. He has an outlook that Earth is changing from the way it is and let's hope that its existence will always be here as a wondrous resource for the world and human beings.

Thereby close here, he is sensing the forces and etherealizing on this Earth. He kindly encourages its preservation so that it existential is continuum which is why he seeks to nature the questions replied not with groping answers but with certainty and assurance. Earth is a place that he continues to strive and add on to its superstructures and city. He leaves this with you the imperishable ground of its sprawling landscape let Earth rest through the day and nocturnal when the soul is vested. It is predominately thoughts; he can think it out whether it is to be a beautiful place and the place before us is beautiful if it is how he perceives it. Happiness is striving and this he has done most perpetually that there is climbed from decadence/ *luxurious self-indulgence* and deprecation/*disapproval* of life impassable.

There is twilight beyond the city, in the auric field of the metropolis the city closes and the sun descends the distant horizon shining pellucid/*translucently clear* over the city onto the screen glass buildings reaching into the sky.

Handle was out to exterminate the pigeons and to save herself from frigorific. The whole night it was being a ruffian and there are cooing of pigeons as mostly being associated with strutting and fighting in male birds. Handle quiet the cooing of the pigeon by culling it. Death comes quickly. The sounds from the loquacious pigeon are exterminated and the bird lay dead on the side of the gravel street.

Afterwards, she dragged the ax inside and welcomed it back to a humid atmosphere. Handle felt sanguine/blood once more running through her body when she has been able to exterminate them like the time you feel when you didn't have to shout vituperation and verbigeration any longer and now you can have yourself again. It is the feeling of no longer lingering. Let not it affect us by killing the adjunct. It is harm free and you can get a good laugh! It becomes heuristic and gets them to shut their coo. Handle was solipsism. The plenum was quiet.

Later, Handle went outside once again because she had heard the cooing and decapitated one of the pigeon's heads. It wouldn't stop cooing. Handle has been patient but after numerous distractions the system has irritated Handle and it seeks commination outside. Subjugation, she has to let it out somehow before it strickens/*troubles.*

Decussation

"The weather makes me tired," says Wian. "Whenever it's gloomy and blithe I can't take the auric field overcasting the skyscraper. It's just ominous."

On any day, Wian would only feel good verve if the sun is out. When it is cloudy he likes to remain indoors. Wian enjoys sunny weather, but he admires all weather.

Adam studies with Wian and is his faithful student from the very beginning. Adam has the symptom of hallucination and dealt with it like Lux stemming from difficulty with language acquisition from childhood. They were both remedial students.

Since Adam was an orphan, adopted at age five he was slow in speech. No one taught him at a young age. Though we all acknowledge like everyone in the universe one one can talk. Speaking requires a lifetime to perfect like anything else. Especially speaking we need to attend to.

Wian likes Adam Clive when he saw the child from the beginning because the child stands out and wanted to follow Wian, Wian grew attached and decided to sign paperwork to adopt Adam when he had not yet met Alice. Wian likes being charitable if he can.

Like the symptom that possesses Lux, Wian

studies Adam and tries to discover what caused Lux to be labeled insane and maybe hallucination fueled it. How is his circumstances extenuating for Alice to want him acquitted? This is for Lux to get the best of this punishment.

Wian was cogitating when Adam walked in.

Hallucination is when one sees or hears thoughts that are delusional, telling it lies. The subject however normally cannot differentiate between real and unreal. Because they hear prolonged noises it abducts and subverts them to think what the noises saying are real. Patients lose touch of reality and think that a delusional world of hallucinating thoughts is existing. Really?

Hallucination is different from telepathy and it all has to do with the power of the mind. Insertion of thoughts and hearing noises by another mindscape of someone else exists.

What we have to tell differences here are the noises in our mindscape delusional versus mind link that is the power of the mind, known as telepathy.

People who are schizophrenic and recover can have telepathic powers and become geniuses. They do not decompensate and lost track of mental steadiness and eventually the noises off the wall subsides.

"Hi Adam, how are the noises treating you? Have they gone away?"

"Mr. Brown, I think I am about to recover. You

are much of a help during this time when you would have endless conversations with me to improve language acquisition in my cortex. You are like a therapist so that I would keep in touch with reality. I had someone here with me all the time throughout because of you. You keep telling me to quit hearing these noises off the wall. There were many noises of different people, but I don't know who they are. Maybe they just sounded like someone we know but not."

"Lux claims he hears these noises too and he undergoes hallucination. I don't know if there is enough evidence to believe it. Lux seems sly. Why can I let him get away with insanity? That cannot be extenuating, I cannot let him get away. I don't want to know Lux's circumstances. He is a doltish to raid the hospital and causes Alice's death in place of mine. There is no extenuation to Lux, insanity does not cut it."

Wian decussated/X out Lux. The bigger X atop the little Lux x.

Lepidoptera Three

"Lux embarked on a train railing to put his
psyche and conscience into revelation.
Ratiocination is healing."

"He has committed a crime. God would only
accept him when he has sacrificed penance and be
punished."

The Train Railing

Somehow it brought him from afar to where the
textile has been manufactured. He said he is on a
mission to extirpate the spreading of the moth's eggs
that are a cause of allergen. He rides through the
countryside having the musings in the valence of his
mind though has been trying to stay sobriety at the
scene of the railing. The train is derailed. From the
window the passengers can speculate the motion of the
moving train. Once it starts to rain the sounds of it
droplets can be heard on the roof of the train. The
train has been in motion. Out in the valley is the mass
of evergreen that jut upward in the sky. It covers the
mountain ranges that are majestic and spacious in the
open land field arena. He passed by the evergreen
mountain ranges and the vibe is renascence. It is higher
up in elevation but he is not acrophobia/*fear of height* and
does not have fear of subverting. The emerald valley
persisted for miles until he entered a different terrain.
While he is there he is claustrophobic because of the
elevation that the railing has to traverse. The air became

humid for an interval because of its elevation and then when he drove past it, the air became immaculate again. He travels across the green valley to see the green side of nature. It is serene except for the sounds of the train. There are sections of mists when the plenum appears with fog and the road ahead at the margent. The drive mandated the lights be turned on though it is during the day time so that he could make out the road. There are green mountains on either side of us and he travels in between.

It is by noon time when lunch is served again. Lux has ordered a light lunch that is brought out to their station in almost the same manner. Again the silver top and the viands served on a large platter. The viands in the train are commonplace. They have a sumptuous menu. It is now morning and the first hue of nature has irradiated effulgently from the distant horizon that seemed as though it was in front of us when he passed by its natural terrain. The shadow of the ramose on the tree is casted against the natural light and the sun looks as though it is in front of us. The orange light of the train lights up anytime he is headed to a destination to pick up new passengers. The train made frequent stops either to load new passengers, drop off passengers or switch drivers and staff on board. The train made several stops within the two hours we boarded. By the time it is 8 o'clock most of the passenger seats from three steeples are occupied.

The chef on board has just started the kitchen and Lux ordered their continental breakfast served with coffee. It took only a few minutes before the server returned with his order on a large platter cover with a silver top. She opened the top as though presenting the meal and then it was served. It has been a long night and he has decided to take off to find remedy for the malady. In his heart, he is to seek the medicine man Wian and he would be able to help cure his psychopath. He knows Wian would be there.

He has to venture here to fix matters before timing is off. He has acted now to secure a revolutionary future as there have been many emblems and recidivism. He has to catch himself succinctly before the polices' investigation becomes hindrance. He has not meant to hurt anyone, it must be the psychotic symptoms.

It is the first appearance of precipitation this season and it is expected that it would be continuum. There has been aberration and the celestial has precipitated sooner than expected. It is sentient to tell that the wind is strong and it is coming from various directions hence the rain switched direction. The sounds of the rain and wind are not jaded by the sounds of the train engine. He is on an imperative excursion that needs to take place immediately. The sounds of the rain echoed sonorously. The rain droplet and hail hitting the metal substance of the train causes echoes. The rain continued to drizzle throughout the day and its sound was heard from the inside of the train. It rains the entire night and seldom it stopped and the sun would reappear. The rain would shine effulgently and cast its reflection on the raindrop forming multicolor of the rainbow. Later it would continue to rain and then there are intermittent when the sky would clear out completely and the sky would be cloudy but clear of rain. Ratiocination is the healing. There are ways of obtaining illumination. He has to traverse there. Lux has derailed. On the exodus, from the morning adret and towards crepuscules he is anticipating signs of discomfiture and menace.

Sometime on the road when he travels he has revived and the reality of it is time on vacation away from these cumbersome thoughts that he is able to have Ratiocination lucid and not be hindered by its miasmatic and allergen. He can be away from the problem or is he running away from it when he has been certain to be right and all they tried to do is infiltrate him with noisome. Where he headed on province somewhere, he has been outlandish and the road never stops to keep going for eternity. Does it run out? He wonders if Ratiocination has heard the news or has the world heard of the recrimination from his conscience.

We are on the road and learning every lesson and lore. It corrals him along the road on the immense world as the train is moving forward. He has cogitation of the past and the paragon tomorrow when he arrives, now perhaps he would have peace. He is free and no longer at an impasse in the predicament of oppression. He is transcending from this point insofar that the past is not to be an obligation. Maybe after the interval would be ultimate he would defray/*pay* everything. He is no longer in the Neolithic chamber for the land is outstretched before him and there are great expanses before the road. The land can continue for a long time without a destination where he would direct. He would be stuck in an engirdling bricolage/*creation from a diverse range of available things*, of an abyss where the pathway subtending is impasse.

His will is to be free. He can begin life anywhere free from verbigeration/*gibberish*, there is no need for a fight. Life on the pathway somewhere made him vicious when he was against the tide. This has given him rictus/*grimace*. When he has not battled off these corruptions and restives he would truly find happiness and not have to ratiocinate these unnerving thoughts he has been running off. He is pushed to the edge of insanity. Will he make it? How to kill the moth people whether they are subjects or objects of the crux. The moth people are a type of people who believe in their personal power. This is the eponymous/*named after something* of the lepidoptera and it is the nocturnal moths that have incinerated the massive soma.

Now he has thought, somehow it is in a dream, he has been convicted before time runs out. He must venture to another venue where the plant spirits will save his soul from penetration and infiltration if his prayer is to be answered. There is always negative energy so that he would be at antagonism and animosity negative energy are not splendid and cause him lag and befuddle. They are irradiating energy un sacra and making the atmosphere miasma when they fight evil which he can be reluctant to, if he finds himself peace and serenity.

He is traveling to see land and more land keep coming up the extramural. It seems as if he is never going to reach the end of it. They are going to infinity, negative energies generate sniffles. The system keeps coming up with banter to obstruct their smoking to make the situation perplexed. He has thought daily when he is going to reach acme/*the highest point*. He kept climbing and they kept pushing him down.

Illumination is not impunity. He must go here to carceral to expiate he thought. No matter what, he is not to condone his behavior. He has committed a crime. God would only accept him when he has sacrificed penance for his misgivings/*doubts*. So that he would regain conscience and not let heretic and insanity beget him.

He has been thinking while on the railing of the prospects in life. Which road his life has partaken its sprawling when he would be back in the city. He would not take long when he returns, he has promised himself of this and has been peremptory/*domineering*. It tries to belittle compared to who we are through demeaning/*belittling* and he can not help it but grasp animosity. He has also noticed the antithesis that he matters only so little compared to the gargantuan universe; he comprises the vulnerability of only one person juxtaposed with everything else there is in the world. The Earth is recondite/*little known* in a manner that one person cannot make a difference but one person can be indispensable/*cannot be without*.

He does not comprehend why there has to be much hatred. Miasma. Miasma. When will the world be enough? While he is traveling profundity/*wisdom* of thoughts traversed. By happenstance/*coincidence* he might see the moth. One summer is not always cogent/*convincing* and he is hallucinating seeing images of lepidoptera. He looks at the years in the past as they were seminal years.

He is now in a different terrain more geographic along the mountains when he is making his stop near the railing. He sees the scene of the mountains among the mountain ranges of the world.

He has been in oblivion but as though seemingly when it is time to derail he has corralled/*gathered* his thoughts to sequester strength for the next stop. He is going somewhere, by agenda wherever life would ramify/spoke into a stage of acme.

He arrived at the city hotel to lodge in for the night before he would be at Ratiocination tomorrow morning. It has been a longiloquence road. When the first hue of light appears nature looks as though it is shadow at dim dawn though he is glad that he is at another place. Much cannot be seen because the first hue of light is luminescence and times there are helical rising enough for the eyes to see. Then nature becomes brighter and brighter when the accessories of nature begins to show. In the garden, are the plants of lotus the lepidoptera are attracted to the lotus because of the lights that emanate from there. First thing in the morning Ratiocination has been awaken at meditation.

He has taken the carriage to see Ratiocination at the Site of Pontification in white. The main duty of the Pontifices was to maintain the pax deorum or 'peace of the gods.' The regulation of all expiatory/*atonement* ceremonials needed as a result of pestilence, lightning, etc. The regulation of the public morals, findings and punishing offending parties. The consecration of all temples, other sacred places and objects dedicated to the gods. The Pontifex Maximus is also subject to several inclinations. If you ever see the object of Pontifex Maximus.

Lux is supposed to be coming today for a visit. They would venture to the bazaar and then in the afternoon he would perform healing. He is instructed to drink the ayahuasca brew that has hallucinogenic properties employed for divinatory and healing so that one would regain energy and power. Lux is hoping to find revelation from the sagest thereby he has traveled afar to seek his musing. Then in the afternoon he is to cook the brew after gathering the ayahuasca plants from the spirits that have been calling. There is the small vendor that sells plant of the vendors sold textile that they have heard rumination of the moth infestation by the larvae eggs. The entire store manufactures these products that are meant to be beneficial for the health. We enter the shop to the smell of the plants and the variety of products that are welcoming to customers. The shops have changed over the years, still there are the vibe of tradition. There is the plant of ayahuasca that has healing qualities to indemnify/*compensate for harm to the psyche.*

The medicine treats the allergen from the moth's scale dust that has stained people's clothing and textile somehow it becomes prevalent/*widespread.* It has infested the furlong of the village.

Some nights it can suck vigor out of the soul during the hour of meditation and it makes him feel weaker and wane. Perhaps it is of mobility and the transition has brought about the healing. It has been there in miasma/*stench* at the venue for a time now and perhaps change might be a definitive. In the past it appeared this way before the demiurge/*universe* has not made sense there is more to the story of the moth how incredible his self-perseverance. A moth has dust that sloughs off of the scale (tiny scales) of its wings when it flies or when it lands. It is for aerodynamics/*the way air moves around things* and thermoregulation/ *heat regulation* It lands on humans.

His soul shall rest, he would not have to baffle them. There is no longer a cri de coeur for the prospect of eternity. The bad spirits out of the underworld let him evade this. He has sensed his vigor vitiate/*corrupted*. There has been unity with the spirits on Earth somehow uniting heaven and hell. Some spirits are the nexus between them if there is such a junction when he has sensed the illumination. He has known that there is hope hovering over him at his outcry, he has no one but himself.

He has spoken to Admonition the sexton at the cemetery how he can rid the devil. He needed strength from subversion therefore he has prayed from the crucifixion that his parents interceded to bless for his sake in the agenda he ever needed it would provide him strength and they would pray to build him strong from temptation of the demon.

Beyond mountains there are the unexplored lands that its extent reaches out to infinity. There is the ocean where its reflection can be seen from above. Where will the road take him if he is a peripatetic/*traveler* when he is on an exodus? It must take him somewhere before he runs out of land and when it does he would meet the sea. The sea has an obscure depth in which it is immeasurable. He does not know the mystery of the sea because he is not its inhabitant like the sea creatures.

The venture into the landscape may take days of exploration, the land is vast and one never knows what to expect. The atmosphere has depth and from the ground to the celestial there is a wide space in between. There are land masses that are plateau and plain. It is a landmass of tombstones. They are of various sizes jutting from the ground. There is space in between in which it separates the tomb from one another for walk space. There are tombstones that have been abandoned for years. No one comes to visit. It is left in desolation with cobwebs and stain. They stop coming by to visit after everyone deceased and there is nobody left of their scion.

As night time falls, the sun sets behind the horizon and the warmth of the day is replaced by the chills of the night when it begins to snow. In the fields of tombstone, it begins to get cold and the stone monument freezes from the chill of the night. By the time night falls the cemetery is completely dark and the reflection of the luminescence is shone off the surface of the stone. Part of the epitaph/*writing on the tombstone* can be seen from the lightning that shone on it. The engraved scripts are made out from the luminescence that shatters its lightning on the tombstone. Then the sounds of thunder and the rain followed. Visitors are not allowed at night after the church closes. The black gate is shut by the gloaming of dusk. There are moths at the cemetery.

Sounds like they are certainly not in his favor. He has tried to block it from internal cohesion. The sounds were verbigeration. It was ceaseless during the night. One night he has not been able to fall asleep and ventures on an adventure to the other side of the chapel to the cemetery. The sounds are coming from there as though the dead spirits are calling out. Somehow he has drawn to the moth because he is curious.

Lepidoptera Four

"What a pabulum."

"Alice forgives him."

It enters the zone of repentance where there lay the misty mountains. When he enters this place it is ethereal and he can be uplifted like heaven to see the view from the summit. He thinks of the misty mountains and how he would be able to start all over again if he would be in prison and then frisson/*thrill*.

By 8 o'clock in the morning Admonition is at the graveyard raking the leaves from the trees that have been falling and accumulated over time. There are matutinals/*mornings* when the fog is plenty and it would blur the entire cemetery space into its cyclone of white cloud, it is blurred and nothing can be seen. He would tell the judge everything. He knows the verdict would be against him They know there is renouncement and self-abnegation.

There is casualty and how many people die per year? The cemetery continues to expand and eventually space runs out, it might have to fill the space from the glades. Lux has been here for meditation when he experienced internal illumination. Usually there is not much that operates at the cemetery. They usually say a prayer and spend time with the soul that is on its journey to depart the world. Some companions spend the entire afternoon in hope of revelation so that they would be abducted from misery and perhaps the spirits would transcend. There is spiritualism about a

106

cemetery, it is the space where the dead are consolidated and they share a common ground. There are the lands of the living and the land of the dead, precinct/*district* from the living world. He has never experienced, when he is foisted/*forced* to not wake up and be bedridden for eternity. He has never experienced the sleep of eternity when sometimes it feels everlasting in the night. He can sense their spirits that languished/*weakened* on this Earth. The mountains are adjunct with mountain ranges in axillary can be looked distal to see the views but the mountains are misty and he cannot see the extramural the moment when the blur can corral his thoughts. He is to reach acme with help, the world has different thoughts and there are various dimensions to be bricoleur over maturation and transformation. Over the misty mountains on the other side is adjunct happiness and adventure pass this rampart/*wall*. Sometimes he is not able to see it but in the utmost moments he will be visionary. He has to traverse to the other side to pass this stunt then he can be condoned/*approved*.

The cemetery space changes with the seasons. Its red leaves have the apperception of fall and soon the leaves will fall and the branches will be barren. Admonition enjoys the afternoon and evening vibe of the cemetery. During the winter time which he anticipates snow will cover the Earth and the landscape is forsaken until the snow mantle melts when spring is renascent. The ground will be covered in frost from the winter snow. This time of year especially when spring has been at the margent, is a pleasant span for visitation. The auric field of spring is in the air and there is the scent of the Taraxacum/*dandelions* are the small flowers collected together into a composite flower head. There is the whirlwind of florets engirdling the air. Lux visited Alice's epitaph and cried to her. He has been glad that she forgave him. He set down the white masterpieces, her favorite and he cried to her.

He has to condone the accident and tell his alibi to everyone. He has no alibi maybe allegation, he has hurted Alice. He has no justification of his where about being at the scene of the crime armed.

"You are insignificant and sinecure. You are pitiful and futile compared to Wian if you don't kill him. He operates the entire Debonair Sanatorim. You are not at parity with him. So show him what happens if someone gets in the way," said Alexander Tanner.

"There is nothing to Wian. Why he is Wian. He is my contrast. I can run that place better than he can. I have better internship than Wian. He is too safe. We have the entourage on our side and following us compared to his cadre. They are followers of his who are mindless and I can operate it better than he can. There is no innovation with him. People do not believe in Wian for a future. I do not believe in Wian. He is a sinner and a cheat. Let him be subdue," Lux antagonized.

"You can't beat Debonair under him. He is more confident than you and your sister is even on his side. She doesn't think anything of you. She pities you that is why he keeps you there as his cadre," said Alexander.

"I am not hearing this and you watch it."

"I can be with you and I will watch what Wian will do. You are going to beat him then yes. We have an alliance. You must kill Wian for me. He looks down on me too. He is always in the way. Rid him then. Do I have your words or do I have to take care to rid Wian on my own. I can send someone else," lied Alexander.

Lux recalls the conversation. It infuriated Lux that Alexander has thoughts of him as pity and sinecure. He thought to Admonition.

"I do not believe in Wian. I am more confident than Wian, he cannot compared to me. I am more talented than Wian. Alice loves me more."

He is now incarcerated. Alexander has not yet been caught because there was no alibi against him. Alexander is only framed for trickery and brainwashing. The director who sends the order is not the perpetrator therefore he is not responsible, but must pay fines.

He has seen the last of the lepidoptera at dim dawn. It is the last sight of the venue. There is nothing more to this musing some allusion to another self within man; it is of the Secret Pathway and foundation of morality that guides the self to the conscience. *It is part of my purpose to show that such persons go wrong when they make the mistake of accepting the common condition of human mentality as representing its ultimate.* He needed to be in search of new Americans and the existence of a good part of this world that they inhabit. He wanted to explain but no explanations would expiate his comportment/*personality*.

The trains run under wide rivers and through mountains of solid rock that plummet en route as though forebodingly fatal. Once again he returns to civilization the time he has been rusticating and the verve inside of him of euphoric transform inside of him.

This is the exodus of Lux on a journey to heal himself from solecism/*breach*. There is an instinct to harm and to the extreme kill. The government deprecated theoretical systems were bantering against his will in which he has been beating them in the riot but since the incident of the lepidoptera there has been a personality change from cohesion in his visceral. This also a representation of the fracas against the machination of character which if in connection and parallelism has been a discovery. Lux has been careful about the foil of the bureaucratic contravention. Would he let love be his valor and about this aspirant the lepidoptera has drawn him into fracas? He has not wanted to give heed, but the binary is put aside so that the qualm would not appease him. _Lux no longer loves himself and gives his life to carceral in return to Alice. He loves only Alice who sacrificed. What would be an adjunct in this way? He would still be wrong. Pandemonium.

What is happening over the misty mountains? One dare not speak of it or recall. For there is a portent of harm for one is afraid to destruct the harmony. But one day he may venture over there to see what is on the other side and he may find gold. Alice has forgiven him.

The last moment of terminus when he set down every restive and made it final; there is the last breath that he hoped for matters to be right that he may go to heaven or hell this moment. Here at the misty mountains he felt that suddenly he must transcend life and every matter shall obtain its denouement. He is returning himself to peace this moment he pays homage, why then would he worry of it anent tomorrow and save himself from damnation. This moment feels heavy; there are impositions that remind him of his sins that must be put to rescind. It feels burdening at the end where the hardened heart has been perpetrated at infinity. There is a brief moment of truth and ethereality that he is let free of everything and no longer can withhold the lie to himself and internally there is stealth. This moment there is illumination.

There is catharsis/*cleansing,* the soul is relieved and revamp. There is riant smile and cry interchangeably then he reflected and found the soul repentant, till there is internal happiness. His understanding is mammoth, he hoped for the ultimate. At this moment, he is groping for a paragon. He thinks of it in rarity does he not; he would not let peccavi/*guilt* and crime happen to himself standing here, when matter is close to conclusion. He confesses extremity to himself and effuses the script.

Somewhere the world has transit of its weather; the season nature transits its raiment from the color of deciduous tree to hue of red, gold, yellow and brown. It is visible that nature appears older in its no longer nascent colorization of evergreen emeralds. The prowess of the sun shines effulgently and it glistens on the leaves whose pigment of yellow and gold shines brilliantly against the sun. There are days when the sun disappears under the nebulous clouds and nature is hues of tenebrous and gloom. The red leaves brighten the raiment of nature to appear iridescent. From day to day the leaves change their hue of color, nature is calm during this time. There are land masses where there are no inhabitants. The sun sets over the horizon every day and its radiation is casted after crepuscules.

Sounds are the agent that diffraction can traverse through the tympanic membrane passively and cause irritants because of its dialects. It is the night and the street appears different from the inside scope. There is fog early in the morning and still no one has awakened. Nature appears nebulous because these objects are covetous in darkness, the night is silent and serene. Then he moves remote a distance, what can become of him to see the visionary over the misty mountains? The future is undetermined and bountiful; it lays the mysticism that is beyond unfathomed. The future is undecided. The world is as mysterious as it is in the abysmal and its disposition is unfathomed. The future is imminent; he must obtain for himself in the world filled with *possibilities*. When the environment changes it can bring about modification and germination of geniture and earlier on it depicts the agent of change from primordial nascent state to contemporary.

There is not much inspiration to start work for that afternoon because there is lack of concentration but the author in the afternoon has returned from his business of ethereal and is now returning to the stationary after scripting. The house they live in now is their paraphernalia/*personal belongings* that they worked hard for while procuring a living in the new metropolis. What is happening in autumn this time of year compared to the primal when the weather is imbibing the vibe of the city and attenuated with the *colorization of foliage* when the time elapses into late autumn the leaves would be shed from the barren ramifications? What is more there is to be signs of evolution and heave. Definitive over conjecture and exactitude is to be modernized over evasive to further alleviate garrulousness. For on the inside he does not like sounds and he has a fixture for misophonia/*conditions where sounds drive you crazy*. The terror of the night is restless and often there is pain that one tries to evade. This predicament is happening in the autumn passing when he decides to venture on an exodus to another place in which he would be cured from sounds.

It is the rainy season again and it rained, he is up watching the rainfall from the window and the prolonged storm inundate the city. There are blockages on the road because of the natural demolition. The tree branches fall from its intact on the road and cause obstruction of the road. The streets are covered with fallen leaves. There are constant storms and their weather lacks its verve. There is nothing that can be done to change the condition of the weather but harbor with its portent. During the night, he can hear the obstruction and nature made its combat. There are noises of tumult thunder storm and the sounds of crackling woods of broken branches tottering. There are sounds of the swaying of leaves and the hissing of the winds.

There are sounds that he has to evade in order to fall into repose. He thinks the storm continues the entire night and then while he is listening to its tumultuous he falls deep asleep. When he has gained verve it is already morning. Then the inundation of sounds starts he cannot block it out passively, there are sounds of dejection. When death strikes then he must depart the world and transcend. There is prospect of the afterlife yet no one is assured. Last night there were rainfalls and the storm continued. The storm has been ongoing for months now and this winter is prolonged. Whenever there is death there is the antinomy, insignia of birth. The mass is growing every day and there are equally people deceased then people being procreated into the world. He thinks Alice is going to reincarnate and be human again.

In the plenum, plenty of matters can happen and while the other specter is silent he is disturbed throughout the entire night. It has been Neolithic and he has developed the mentality in quiet. While the rain cantillation and echo struck him asunder. The thunder roars and there is lightning and the first event in matutinal there can be a baby born. We have experienced geniture/*birth* again from the afterlife if we can hope for this after our first death, if we felt this moment primal. This is the emblem of every day repose that we never awake. We sleep to the sounds of the rain and etiolate/*feeble* the memories that previously disjointed. It has been traversed and exists in another life somewhere else. There are mishaps in this world that are not abided and the days forthcoming are continuation. He may indite while in carceral.

It looks as though the rain will continue for a time incessantly. Each day happens per diem at a time and then soon he has been remote from the lost island for a few years. There is new social convention per diem and it continues to evolve with the innovation on Earth. The social being makes evolution and they impart changes that reflect humanity. The beauty of the world enlivens with day to day convention life happens and we expect every day. The Earth continues to propagate. The beginning of the day begins with the humid sunrise when there is the hue of light iridescent onto nature. The colors of nature begin to show from its shadow. Piecemeal/*gradual* nature becomes alive and there are insignias of life. The inhabitants of nature disperse; the birds and insects' creep out of its inhabitants by the time matutinal arisen and their day starts. There are days spent working and days in placation, we awake with a purpose.

His senses transcend the misty mountains and not let his heart wane. We cry out illogically in pain for the lack of reasons that the soul is havoc and unsettled, there are reasons that humanity should not fail. For a moment he is not able to see the blur catches his eyes at a glimpse and he might not see the entire picture until it is sprawled out before us. He must damn them hell. Has he done it for reasons? How has he lived life to have meanings? It transpired that there is definition in sinecure now and pabulum/*bland*. He ponders the question if there is an afterlife and if it exists, does it desist in the realm.

Many generations ago it is still totemic and its

wisdom has been so far but a disposition for fame. In conclusion it is a conative for personal power to rid it in the midst of chaos. Finally, the lepidopteran has made it. He can already see the horizon on the other side. There is reversion and his soul is at peace and he sees the world from a brighter view. Has it all been a dream? Lux has wondered what happened to Alice. The moth has been the effector. *Lux adheres sin to his conscience and somehow not let himself escape.* The incident happened so rapidly last night from the crux of the diurnal. It has not made sense to him and he consulted Admonition. It has been the sequence of events that happened. Now the luminescence suspended over the night. He has to figure out why he has been having dreams of Alice and he has been in carceral. When he was awakened he was incarcerated.

In the nightmare he hovers over the body that infuriated him. The body is dead now the polices have reacted. This morning is quiet as though nothing happened. Before he took off at dim dawn he had seen to it that it was all darkened and the lamp was off. The moth has told the constable otherwise. The same dust scale that they found on the white shroud is the same residue on the counterpane that is over Lux. It has been enigmatic and has no existence in a dream. He has been Alice. Perhaps she has taken his character away or so it appeared. It has not been his sister. He killed his character when she passed away because of him.

Now that he is up it seems as though everything is a nightmare or some type of dream. This is questioning and the verdict to be promontory no matter what the situation has called or recount the outcome. They are

Lepidoptera people, and it has been questioning what has happened to Alice. Is hard to believe over the prosecution he wanted to believe, Lux has escaped on extenuating circumstances before the polices can get to him for the alibi to decipher who has killed the body of Alice. Somehow he is incarcerated and he remembered that he has taken off going to the Dominican Church in the back of the cemetery.

The details are untangling, the moth foretold to the polices the killer, the acts are traced and evidence shown. He remembered being algific/*cold producing* and pallor/*pale* and stuck out in the snow.

He has sensed his mysterious overself acting descent in the moments of detriment evil. They find man a paradoxical being; one capable of descent into the darkest abysses of evil. He has supplicated for himself to live and his conscience to live. He has wanted vitality. Let not his conscience be possessed. He has wanted strength and really he has lived. Let someone hear him. There is illumination to save him.

He leers into the oblique to see the ambulance and the cordon dissipates until either sight or sound is out and into thinness of dust. No more flickering of lights and loud rebarbative noises as the vehicle traveled down the ribbon of asphalt to his arrest. This terminal is eternal if there is eternity there is the best moment when he has been justified and given freedom and rights.

Now he sensed that everything is copacetic and he whiteout.

It is ironic. The moth is irony. In which its symbolism and perspective he has speculated. He keeps seeing the lepidoptera in the carceral and has dreams of it. It is irksome and he has killed some. It has not been his intention to be at ascent against being the hapless prey of time…pabulum. He serves ten years. *Alice forgives him.*

He thought of Alice terminus; he would never move on from it. He would never let her go. For several years he has dealt with this qualm in which he has navigated his way around its savage to beat the giant monster eponymous of tyrannous. He has hope of recrudescence on Earth as the sun descends after crepuscules and to save himself like he has supplicated. There need not be crime, abuse, rape and homicide as these are essences to the verve of the psychedelic sociopath as hedonist/*pleasure seeker*, a means of significance. His mentality is distorted to be fraught/ *full of* hedonism. He contemplates himself and does not know what deluge in him as a criminal and life is off track before he reached culmination. He feels himself a criminal but he knows he must be sentenced. Has he been tenuous? It has been the breach of society truly comprehensible that there is euphoric in commination/*vengeance* if they by force oppress him, is it the hapless prey of time before he becomes explosive. He can withstand a 10 year sentence. He hears his own laughter seldom against their grim reaper. He has speculated on criminology and motive of hedonism and strange ideas and tells Alice why he has only been happy that he gets to repent. There have been moments he has laughed and suddenly he would cry of missing

Alice.

THE TWILIGHT OF EACH DAY

"TWO FLOCKS OF BIRDS WENT THEIR SEPARATE PATHWAYS
SUBTENDING THE SKYLINE."

"IT IS EVENING."

Wian and Charmaine went to the Jewelry shop where Alexander might be found because he is a jeweler. Wian went in disguised as a girl in case Alexander recognized him. They are out to get news of Damian. They accosted Alexander there.

"Do you know Damian? I was an old friend of Damian."

Surprised to Charmaine, Alexander said "I do know Damian. He is an attendant here. What do you need, little one? What can I do for you? Damian has lost all of his memories from the past. He was injured in an accident." He paused. "He is with a girlfriend. She is my daughter Amy. She is around your year. And you are?" Alexander turned his attention to the tall woman Wilma and glanced at her plump faux bosoms. "Did you need help selecting these diamonds or gold? Diamonds are forever. You pick her choice my lady...perfect for a pretty gal like yourself."

Alexander said gesturing to the diamond with the best cut that shines and stands out. "Your height is paramount like these diamonds girl."

Wian cleared his voice to notch it up an octave

and replied, "Maybe we will come back another time. We don't mind gold though. Never diamond. Diamond is luxurious though some can be tepid. That one is way too shiny." Wilma flicked her lashes, worried to be found at incognito.

Charmaine was astounded and impressed of Wian but intercepted, "Do you know where we can find Damian?"

"Watch out for him at Club Z at night." And turned to Wilma. "Brilliant, you are one, smart doll." He motioned and gestured for them that they were free to take off.

Alexander shook his head at the awkward encounter. The company of two egress from the jeweler shop and anticipated their nocturnal adventure.

That night Wian and the two twin girls went to Club Z trying to find Damian. The neon lights from the club were dispersed throughout and the fluorescent halo lights were reflected on the people sitting at the bar counter. The company was at the lounge and there they spotted Damian walking in front after prowling the entire night. Charmaine came over to Damian and they got close and both gazed into each other's eyes by coincidence.

"Excuse me," he said after a while. "You're in my way."

"You don't remember?" said Charmaine.

"I'm sorry miss, I already have a girlfriend."

Charmaine was frozen and returned to her seat at the lounge chair.

"He does not remember a single thing or not," Charmaine said, frowning.

Einstein went over there and tried to say hello.

"Hey, I just saw you at the entrance in a different outfit. I already said I have a girlfriend. You slu…"

Einstein covered Damian's mouth. "I am not. Do you know me? Of course not. If you don't remember. Charmaine is your girlfriend. That is my twin. She's right over there."

There is a flashback of someone who looks like Einstein when she intonates the name Charmaine. Damian grabbed Einstein's elbow and pained her. She hit him on the head by accident, with a hard plow.

"I remember, I know you." Damian said and lost balance and he was inundated with a migraine and almost collapsed when Charmaine came next to him in time to hold him up. He was knocked out and unconscious.

"Charmaine…Charmaine…" he muttered. Am I seeing double? This migraine is getting worse. How can there be two of you?"

They took him over to the lounge area and explained to him each dragging either side.

They splashed ice cold water from the bar into his face and it awoke him. He was startled when he awoke with his hands tied into a noose behind his back. Wian did that just in case he escaped from them since his identity was altered. Wian's main concern is why Damian is an assassin. For their protection Wian had tied his hands in a knot that was entangled and took experts to disentangle. Damian awoke and struggled trying to remove the knot but was incapable.

"Listen to me Damian. I am not trying to harm you. These are my daughters. They are apparently twins. We need you to stop it? Are you getting me? Stop being an assassin. This is my daughter Charmaine. And you knew her in the past and you two were close friends."

Charmaine came next to him and asked "Do you remember us?"

"I remember vaguely now. I think Charmaine got me back or something hard hit me in the head."

"Or both," said Einstein.

"No, we never slept. I didn't sleep with Amy," said Damian.

"That is Alexander's daughter," said Charmaine.

"How did you know? I am sorry I did kissed

another girl," Damian confessed and looked away.

Charmaine was teared but looked away also so they couldn't tell. But they all heard.

"Let's discuss this matter later. I hope the trouble is over, do you remember everything?"

"Yeah, Mr. Brown."

"First off, I'm glad you're back on our side now. There are brighter days now and not night. Alexander is the culprit, not you, so don't worry. He had brainwashed you and trained you to become an assassin. Secondly, it's exonerated by me but we are truly contrite and sad. It is indelible tainting on your character and I don't think we can accept you or you can get it back. It is sad to your reputation," said Wian shaking his head of disapproval though in sorrow looking down.

"I want you to make it up by volunteering for community services and charity from now on and on. Do good deeds if you can and whenever there is anyone who is in need of help you should make yourself available. I show deep condolences to you about my daughter's feelings. She will never be able to look at you the same."

"What about Uncle Lux? How come you wouldn't acquit Lux?" asked Einstein.

"Lux darkest intention pressured by Alexander was to murder me. I know Lux didn't like me either.

Alice is gone because of Lux. He deserved to pay. By the way, Lux wants to pay anyway because that is who he is. That pabulum is shit."

The next morning is a new dawn, a new day and Damian is back with them. The sun is already out by sunrise but the temperature is cold. There is frost on the grassroots and rime on the branches of the maple trees outside. It was his first day back and everything is anew now from the harrowing past. Damian needed to catch them up with everything.

They were at the courtyard of Debonair Sanitarium talking on one cozy day. They each got a hot mug of hot cocoa or hot milk tea to relish in from the cold. It is December, the end of the year and the coldest month.

Charmaine wanted to talk to Damian about each other. She knew it was going to be strickening. She can tell that he was unhappy too. But she was glad that he still picks her to be with them and on the good side.

"I apologized for my relationship I had with Amy. She was always there with me from the beginning to take care of me, but I never forgot you."

"I can't forgive you Damian, because I am a good girl. And my dad would never want it either. They already know I celibate and never marrying. I think he had talked it over with mom. I don't think we are the same. I cannot look at an assassin and think the same of you. I know it is not entirely your fault but you acted on it and I think you're a bad person but not a murderer. It is in your will. But I know you were brainwashed. You shouldn't have killed anybody. You can't go back now."

"I don't mean to hurt you. I am not a murderer. If there is anything I can say to make it better for us I would but I am not a murderer. I am deeply remorseful and expiatory and will try to fix it and make it up."

"Why did you kill anyone and became their assassin? Charmaine teared up but looked away and down.

With Damian being back, Charmaine is meagerly happier knowing that he is on the good side and that they are going to take down Alexander. Charmaine wants to be like Wian so her predilection would be someone like her Dad who knows good from evil. She was glad Damian is restored for him and it must feel like renascence, a rebirth.

She was completely understanding of him but she was not able to accept him. She feels disgusted sometimes that he committed a crime. How can someone actually be ruthless enough to abduct the life of another human being like themselves. His hands are full of blood and stained. Charmaine cannot love a gruesome murderer. Maybe time will change in despair. He understands and waits for her.

Charmaine doesn't enamored anybody but her family. In a platonic way she adores Damian. But in a carnal way she cannot accept Damian again because she suspects he is closer to Amy. Charmaine never consummated with Damian to celibate and keep her pageant. There was no way she would accept him now after not wanting him before anyway. Because of Damian it confirms Charmaine's celibacy, she was very happy there is no reason to not. When she thinks about Damian she would get sad. Now, she would get to keep her virginity for the rest of her life and all the time remain pageant.

Everything happens for a reason. Damian must have shared a lot of first time with Amy. That is why it bothers Charmaine meagerly. From then on, Charmaine and Damian share platonic love. Whenever he gets close physically she becomes suspicious if he has done it with Amy. That remains the reason for their fight for the rest of their lives together. Time gradually changed how Charmaine viewed Damian. Maybe he was just brainwashed and had no intention of hurting humanity.

Wian said "We thought you celibate anyway, Charmaine, your mother and I. You should feel right that way. I hope you are alright. Choose what your conscience tells you. Your thoughts, not feelings, are the guiding light."

ALONE TOGETHER

Wian is forever with the apparition of Alice after she deceased. Somehow Alice is looking down from heaven and thinking to him. Their thoughts are mindlink. Anytime he wants to conjure Alice he would think of her and she would be able to hear it and reply. Maybe this is just in his imagination. She is living in heaven and he is living on Earth and somehow they are connected to and part of each other's world. We are not mindsets apart but one mind together. Though you are invisible and not present.

It was sometime in December, the end of the year that was Alice's funeral. They kept the body preserved for a time in the morgue and transported it to the cemetery on one Monday afternoon. Wian spoke a eulogy to Alice at the funeral.

To my beloved Wife Alice Aeterna Brown:

Ever since the first day I met you, you have been a person of sententious. Not any of us are more righteous than you. You are beautiful and have a beautiful soul towards myself and everyone who has met you would never ever question your kindness. It is always only you who can de jure me. You beat me in reason and this time again. This last time. I know to this very moment that I promised you I will take care of Lux. Wian searched Lux in the crowd being manacled by his own will and by choice he did not struggle. In the end, I will take care of him, Wian announced. For Alice's worthy heart.

Lux wanted to say something to Alice. Lux was unleashed and allowed to step up to the podium to give his last words. His eulogy for Alice as well.

"I am sorry Alice. He said in cri de coeur. I told you I am a good person Alice. But I truly did wrong to you. I am weak, but I talked to my conscience and I tried. I really want to try Alice. I'm glad you forgive me and I know you will always, loving one. I am going to go Alice to a place to be at so that I can make myself worthy like you. I am going to turn myself in to the police. I am not someone who deserves your mercy. I am stupid." He knelt down next to Alice's sarcophagus and hugged her body close and sobbed. "Take care Alice."

The police came to surround Lux. Lux was under arrest. He was handcuffed again and taken away looking back at the funeral procession. Judge Beth stepped in to stop them.

"You're not going to honor the dead one at her funeral? We're just going to handcuff Lux? Let's not execute until after it's over. What an imbecile. At least you turned back around. We're here Lux." said Judge Beth.

Lux passed by and looked downward. Too remorseful and ashamed of his action to look at Wian in the eyes.

Then Alexander showed and looked down at Lux. Lux struggled from his manacle to set himself free to pulverize Alexander but was tied down. "You go to hell bastard! Son of a dog!"

Alexander laughed in hedonism and disappeared forever.

The ceremony continued and the pallbearers interred the coffin into the ground as the crowd all cried out in remembrance of Alice taking off forever. After she was interred they threw the tripod flowers on top of the soil. The engraved epitaph was 'A White Promise.' With a black and white picture of Alice placarded onto the tombstone. There were many solemn faces in the audience who were cadres, and faculty at the sanatorium, and their relations. Wian was solemn. The rest of the audience had their heads down feeling condolences for Wian whose wife passed away young. If she was meant to live till centenarian, fate had departed her early. It is most poignant when the dead one is young compared to the death of an old age person because it is against nature.

Wian cherished every memory of Alice and himself. The sun ray shines brilliantly against Alice's tombstone and there were spokes emanating from it. "I know you are at a safe place because heaven is with you. Did you see the spokes of sunlight Alice? Are you telling me that you are well?" Wian was speaking to himself with the apparition of Alice. He has sensed her apparition ever since she has died. He can still hear her in his thoughts and forever it will be there.

Wian was the last person at the funeral by evening, night time had not fallen. We can see in the surrounding the white masterpieces growing in groves. It felt like snow in December in the villa they reside in. Alice's voice echoed in his head.

Nine years later, Wian is now at retirement age. They never were able to forget Alice's presence every day of their lives. She had made such a difference in Wian's life up to the very last words.

"It is only now that we are separated but I will see you again the next time. Kismet cheer up. Remember my white promise," said Alice's apparition.

"The promise is done, Alice. I will fulfill my promise to you. I will take care of him after he gets out of prison. I promise to rebuild him all over again."

*Read The Lepidoptera along with Song *"Requiem for a Dream"* by Lux Aeterna.

MY GREAT GRANDPA AND JUDGEMENT DAY

THE PROPHECY

There is nothing yet of the city. But the city today is drenched in the rain. There are many passersby with black parasols over them.

I am writing this in my room on the fifth floor and I can look down from the window when I am awakened to see the people walking back and forth. The city is still and quiet.

I had my lantern turned on and the room gave off a yellow glow from the incandescent bulb. I can see the rain from the veranda dripping downward.

Later on during the evening, there was torrential rain and the ground shook from the making of thunder. I am inside my room hidden from the rain, writing and praying. I hope the rain will not inundate. Sometimes the rain sound is gruesome and it gives off fright. The yellow light elicited warmth and the thermostat was turned up high so that the rain air would dissipate, replaced by air generated by the heater. It was thunderous and the rain was consistent and flooded the first floor.

I didn't go out and stayed indoors because of such an occurrence and I have to catch up on my commission. Writing was proliferating during the time of rain, as I have said powerful words give positive results. My commission was trying to produce a splendid piece of artwork in the midst of the rain while I am stuck on the inside and not able to jaunt outside in the street. My symptoms sojourned and I had to find ways to rid the symptoms of hallucination and the external voices in which I conferred while listening to the rain.

While indoors, I prayed to Jesus. Jesus was a righteous and religious man. Though the Jews denied him as God and because of his claim to be God, they upheld the Sanhedrin Court to crucify Jesus to the cross. While I read these words, thunder came across the sky and gray clouds were inundated. Are we here to make up for our sins in the last life? It feels like the apocalypse, that Jesus shall return to Earth to judge the living and the dead. Eschatology is the part of theology concerned with death, judgment, and the final destiny of the soul of mankind.

I prayed to the Lord. Seek and you shall find, ask and you shall receive, knock and the door shall be opened. I wonder when Jesus will be here. May his kingdom come and his will, will be done. It is by God's will if destiny is to resolve. God will answer our prayer what he thinks is best. There is a raison d'etre behind what ought to happen.

I pray for a story to tell to do well in my writing for God to shine on me with his brilliance. Then the idea came to me while I was praying.

I watched outside where there were people holding up a procession in the rain. That was why there were all the black parasols. There was a procession from the Lutheran Church next to the apartment for a funeral. Someone had passed away in this gloomy weather and there were people in the rain holding black parasols following the hearse which was driving slowly. Then they retrieved to their own transport to shield from the rain.

Then the idea came to me of a character who encountered Jesus. It was during a storm.

This weather is cool and there is rain constantly. Thunder echoes overhead and getting anywhere there are obstacles. Why would anyone be having a procession? It must be someone dignitary for many people to show.

I live next to a Church though it was not the Church I attended, I never looked into it because they were Lutheran and I am Catholic. I am devout to Jesus and pray to him daily. Jesus wants me to do well and he sends me this idea of a Man who asked Jesus about the Rapture. He wanted the rapture to be here.

There was a man named Matthew Benjamin Pham in a tux, treading on the street no longer knowing why he was here after the funeral of his nonagenarian Great Grandpa and he wondered when the end of the world would be. He has so much time remaining, what is he going to do without his Great Grandpa? He thinks of precepts and the dogma and ponders where his Great Grandpa is taken after death. He does not think his Great Grandpa can be dead or there must be something mystical behind this fantod/*unreasonable* when he has revelations.

He is not yet meant to die till centenarian by his prophecy, but somehow his Great Grandpa is fallacy. Morbid, he wants to be united with his Great Grandpa for more of their escapade where will his life lead to now with no stewardship/*supervisor*?

He writes letters to Jesus of the Rapture as he believed Great Grandpa can be living again when the Lord will be here so that he will be united with his Great Grandpa. He asked for the Rapture to come.

I pray to the Lord. Seek and you will find, ask and you will receive and knock and the door will be open.

The weather is trenchant and the storm is coming on. I had left the window open for the cool breeze to get inside the room from the net of the window again. Sometimes when it rains diagonally, rain filtered through the sieve causing rain water to wet the objects in the room.

I will continue writing after lunch. Like Matthew Benjamin Pham, this is all that I did when he had nothing to do on hand in the story.

"God Speak to me!" said Matthew. "Why did you have to take my Great Grandpa away?"

He was dispensing the fantod.

"Who would I have to speak to now after my Great Grandpa is gone? I want you to tell him I need him alive. I am without anybody now in this world.

Jesus please hear my prayer for my Great Grandpa to come back alive and be with me," said Matthew.

He was sitting on a bench outside and the sky began to rain down.

"What is this? Jesus, are you crying for me? That is why you are sending tears?" asked Matthew. "I want you to make my Great Grandpa alive again or make it be judgment day. Can you, Jesus? I do not want to be without my Great Grandpa."

The sky responded and there were echoes of thunder and rain torrentially.

Then he thought of writing to Jesus. How he would make all of this be real that there was no way his Great Grandpa's prophecy could have turned out to be a fallacy. He would still have at least ten more years to live. He had made plans with his Great Grandpa that he was going to live. Now what would he do without his Great Grandpa.

Thunder roared when he let his cortex think of the end of the world. There is something unique the way we cogitate and natural disposition follows like thunder and lighting. This is called nature. Somehow can nature and the earth be controlled?

Once upon a time, there was a myth that there is someone who is the creator of rain existing on earth. And the creator of rain happens to be my Great Grandpa. He created rain from the construction of his brain map. When there was rain we would know that it was my Great Grandpa's doing. The human brain is extremely smart and maybe intelligence gets you to be that way and be able to create rain. That was what I thought when I was young. Somehow the universe is controlled by my Great Grandpa's brain and really the globe shape of the earth is my Great Grandpa's cortex. He can rain down upon us anytime we want I think and end droughts on this earth. There is an area in the head near the pineal gland that is unique of this germline and it is only this family that can inherit the trait of rainmaker. I thought I must work arduously so that I can become the next rainmaker. Therefore I kept speaking to build my intelligence and enlarge my brain space.

When I grow up I want to become a rainmaker like my Great Grandpa and inherit his traits. This was the inspiration I had to work arduously to become smarter so that I can become the next rainmaker. There was only one rainmaker that existed for a time and this trait is possession of our family inheritance. My Great Grandpa had told us this story and he was a great storyteller and I want to emulate him.

Years from now when I am coming of age and I look up in the sky I still wonder if there really was the rainmaker or if it was a myth told by my Great Grandpa when he was living. Can it be an effect created by human's emotions or intelligence, versus nature?

"Jesus you must reply for the end of the world to be here. I want rapture to be here Jesus I have nowhere to go now," said Matthew just returning from the funeral.

Without his Great Grandpa he would not have his escapades and he was already feeling lugubrious in the meanwhile after the funeral. If only there was a way for his Great Grandpa to be living again. It is by God's will. Matthew did not want to let go of a chance to be with his Great Grandpa again and held on to the possibility of a rapture maybe occurring sometime soon or tomorrow. Then he would see his Great Grandpa again and he would be alive again and they would have each other to commingle like old times.

Matthew had spoken a beautiful eulogy at the funeral about his Great Grandpa and he had not shed a tear thinking of his Great Grandpa because he knows that somehow his Great Grandpa is still living.

It had been several hours when he had been doing nothing after the funeral still thinking of his Great Grandpa's prophecy. When it was time to die then you just died, but he had not predicted it. It must be by God's will, but then why did God mandated this? Matthew did not want to be without his Great Grandpa and spoke to the Lord. He is going to write letters to Jesus and send it to an address. If there was an address for Heaven. He didn't want it all to end yet because his Great Grandpa was the main character. What would happen to the story when he dies? Nothing else would happen and this earth can cease to exist. He wanted more events and more time. It has not been enough and we can't just forget where the main character goes but continue to talk about it. All he can do is continue living the legacy that his Great Grandpa passed on.

"Jesus, hear my prayers and bring my Gram back to me. I cannot do without him. Let there be judgment day now," said Matthew.

He looked up in the sky like the clouds immersing overhead as though he was part of the sky. Rain water poured all over him but he did not care. He cried out to Jesus for the occurrence of why he had condoned this to transpire. Great Grandpa was always with him and they were setting out on their mission today to do something else. There was no way he would depart abruptly without Matthew even knowing.

He did not have time to think about it because he had just departed from the funeral and all these events kept occurring. After resting, he now has time to himself so he can think about what was wrong. Was there something odd when he took off? Was there something Gram still wanted done? It can't be the end yet. They were preparing for more adventures today. It was a sudden death. He had wanted a reply from Jesus why he had to mandate this. It was God who had settled this then it is his will, maybe God wanted Matthew to grow and be on his own. Maybe Matthew needed to be by himself. All this must have happened because of reasons and it was for the future. Maybe that is why God had conjured torrential rain. For the end of the world to be here and there would be a rapture. Maybe the sounds of thunder were signals from the archangels and their trumpets. Matthew had thought of it this instance. There was no way his Great Grandpa could have passed away without teleology. I mean he was old, but it couldn't be because they had prophesied it together and he still had another good ten years to live till centenarian.

Matthew was crying now aloud. "Jesus please bring him back to this world somehow. Without him I will be all alone," pleaded Matthew. At this, the sounds of thunder inundated and there were loud echoes.

Matthew continued to cry aloud. "I want my Great Grandpa back!"

Matthew continued to stay out in the rain. He was waiting for something to happen to Earth at the event of his Great Grandpa passing away. Great Grandpa was powerful, when he died, something unnatural ought to happen to Earth. Maybe the appearance of Armageddon or the end of the world.

He was waiting and he kept waiting and didn't care if he was drenched in rain. Something ought to happen now. Something is going to fly out of the sky to speak to him of why this is and his Great Grandpa has to die and be taken away from him. He wanted an answer to this enigma.

What is supposed to happen now is for life to cease to happen and for the end of the world to be here. Life ought to cease to happen when the protagonist dies or something to make the story go along. It has to be in the frame of reference of the protagonist and together they had picked that the main character was his Great Grandpa. How can he know what to do now that his Great Grandpa is no longer here to direct him? He felt lost and delusive. There is nowhere he can go now. What would be his purpose without his Great Grandpa?

"You want me to reach the culmination Great Grandpa, I can't do it without you. I know you're still alive out there hearing this. Please give me an answer," said Matthew.

He knows that death was an eventuation, but he does not know why they were just talking yesterday and now his Great Grandpa has to be taken away from him and he had promised that he would be here. Now all the planning and the dreams of being with his Great Grandpa are shattered. He had gone too soon. They were still going somewhere today in their itinerary.

"I want to follow you, Great Grandpa. Can you hear me? You can't do this to me. Not yet as we have prophesied that you would not be gone yet until centenarian. Where are you now?" asked Matthew.

His Great Grandpa normally shows to console Matthew when he cries, but this time no one shows to comfort him and he is alone.

The next morning Matthew awakened in bed in the warmth of his comforter. It had stopped raining meagerly and then when he awakened it started to drizzle again.

"What happened Jesus? Great Grandpa. Where is he now? Jesus you must tell me where my Great Grandpa is," said Matthew. "Have you prearranged this for everything to happen as is for my Great Grandpa to depart this world?"

There was thunder in the background and the sounds of it echoed in the apartment. Then he got up and wrote to Jesus of his plan to have the rapture happen concurrently so that Matthew would see his Great Grandpa once again.

Dear Jesus,

I want it to be the rapture so my Great Grandpa will be alive again. You shall judge the living and the dead. Please make this happen for the story to continue because you have taken our main character away. Please answer our prayers. I love you Great Grandpa very much. Please take care of him if he is there in heaven with you.

Great Grandpa died healthy. There was nothing wrong with him except he could have lived longer. Matthew thought he didn't expect Great Grandpa to die because we were going to go to the used bookstore the next day and he didn't make it to go with him. The next few days he had to take care of the funeral and had been busy. There was nothing to do without his Great Grandpa and he wished for his Great Grandpa to be alive again. His Great Grandpa normally keeps his appointment, it was abrupt that he decided to depart like that. He is normally good on appointments. He keeps his appointment with Matthew except this time. It was abrupt that he had passed away.

There was a chill in the room and the story was interrupted. Still the rain was consistent and it would not terminate. The rain was getting heavy by the hour. It gave me good ideas for the novel. When I was writing, I would forget about my symptoms. The hallucinations did not come back for a time, until I was free and languorous did it take control of me. The rain sounds were so distracting that it meddled with the sounds produced by the hallucination. Hallucination is hearing unnatural voices in the surrounding that were not produced by an article. I was hearing it like telepathy. Overall there were hallucinations and telepathy. It was there on walls and in the air. I opened the window to let in the rain sound so that the symptom would not disturb me and the telepathy would subside. There were two noises prevalent, the hallucinations and telepathy. Amidst this convolutions, I fell asleep and returned to the dream of Matthew. Later on I continued to write my script again.

"Jesus, please reply. I want my Great Grandpa back now. I would not know how to live without him," said Matthew. Matthew had moved away with his Great Grandpa on their escapadas to college and he lived with his Great Grandpa. Now he is off alone. He doesn't know if he would finish college without his Great Grandpa here. All of a sudden everything must stop. He does not know what to do without his Great Grandpa. They used to discuss it together and he would confer matters in the academic with his Great Grandpa. Now it is the end of it, he wondered why Jesus must do this to him. He knew somehow Jesus had it arranged and everything was going to be copacetic.

When will the rapture be here, Matthew looked forward to the rapture and had asked Jesus for the Rapture to be here this instant so he would not have to deal with it all by himself. He wanted the rapture to be now and his Great Grandpa would be next to him and he would not be alone.

He decided to keep writing his letter and addressed it to heaven or it was omnipotent Jesus would know of it and reply to him. Why his Great Grandpa was taken away from him. He prayed to Jesus. His faith was resilient in Jesus and he did not doubt that one day, now, this instant that there ought to be an answer. Why was Jesus whom he thinks is his Great Grandpa not here with him anymore and when Jesus died isn't that the end of the story? That there ought to be judgment day for his second coming when the living will be united with the dead. He already missed his Great Grandpa who was Jesus.

He took out the letter again and continued writing the letter.

I am writing this to heaven. Please let Jesus who is my Great Grandpa live. I would do anything for this to happen. Please send me Jesus again. I missed the days with Jesus. When he was here, I was strong and resilient. Now I do not know what to do any longer.

He looked outside the window to see if he was somewhere in the celestial or empyrean. Somehow overnight it must have happened and Jesus (the real Jesus) must have called on the earth to judgment and ended the world. One second, he was just inside his apartment and everything was normal except his Great Grandpa was no longer here the next.

I was disturbed. It must be evening now and the rain had stopped for a duration, no one went outside and outside was just normal. Nothing phenomenon happened via Great Grandpa's death so far.

Later I returned to writing my story and Matthew continued writing to Jesus to enforce the rapture so that his Great Grandpa would be alive again and somehow he would be united with his Great Grandpa to learn his lessons. His Great Grandpa always had many visions and insights to conquer them out there. He had many talks for Matthew to learn. Matthew wrote to the empyrean.

I have nothing to do now. I can't do anything without my Great Grandpa, who is Jesus to me. Why was this blessing taken away from me? I don't know why heavenly father you had done this to me. Please reply. Seek and you will find, ask and you will receive, knock and the door is opened. I know the prayers. But now there is still no reply. Jesus I cannot be without you please be with me because I am weak and tenuous. I am afraid without my Great Grandpa who is my guide.

Matthew broke down crying again. You can't do this to me and take away all I have. He cried and then the rain sound created a soporific effect that lulled him to sleep.

There were sounds of thunder and the echoes inundate as though Jesus was replying. There was a voice in the surrounding area that called out Matthew's name. It was Jesus appearing in his dream. It would not be the end of the world. Not now. Not yet. But your Great Grandpa is safe in heaven with the angels. His Great Grandpa appeared with Jesus; they have joined each other in heaven. "Gram!" Matthew went to hug and kiss his Great Grandpa. "Gram! Don't go! Don't go!"

"I am not going anywhere yet. It's Jesus' reply to you. You must live well now without me. Jesus wants you to be by yourself and grow on your own. He is letting you have the chance to grow on your own that is why I am sent away. I am in heaven now living a contented life with the angels and living by Jesus's side. Do not feel saddened for me for I am living a happy life in Heaven and I see the ancestors. Cheer up son. You have a long life to live and do not think of the rapture anymore. It is not yet the time now. There is no Rapture unless Jesus decides it. Eventually it will be time, but you have not graduated yet and you still need to do work on your own to pass your writing and reading classes. I want you to be able to finish college on your own or learn to read, write, and speak to be educated. Education is also moral and ethics, orthodox and cultivation/*formulation* of the self. Much more than the perusal of books, but mainly it. Be educated for the end of the story to be here. You must do it on your own without me here now," said his Great Grandpa Phu.

"What about the prophecies?" asked Matthew

"Life is mercurial, we let God decide it. Truly I want to be there for you. You need to write and read more then I will be here with you. Whenever you write I will be here and answer your questions. God has bestowed me the ability to be humanoid and be here in spirit as an angel. Do not be distracted," said Great Grandpa.

Matthew is moralistic and conscientious. He would not know what to say except when he is with his Gram endless would come to mind.

He awakened. "Gram!" He must be dreaming for the apparition had dissipated. He was glad that he was able to hold his Great Grandpa one last time. He had received the message, but he was in doubt. Maybe all he had to do was continue reading, writing and speaking, that was it. Then his Great Grandpa will be here.

Jesus must have heard his questions and sent the angels and prophets to reply to him. He does not know what to do to go on from here. He rushed to his table and continued writing.

Gram,
I heard you last time. I know you are still here. What should I do now when I have no one to talk to and discuss matters with? I have no one to talk to any longer. How would I ratiocinate it out loud. Therefore I am depressed and dreading this. Please be here for me. I want to finish college, but I am indisposed and ill because I would have no one here for me. Though I hope you are here with me. I know it was your apparition last time. I felt your embrace. What would I

do without you, my love? Thank you for the reminder of finishing my study to be educated. It will not be the same without you. Nothing is ever the same without you. I want you to be here every second. Tomorrow I don't know of tomorrow what will be without you? There are lessons to learn and I cannot do it without you telling me. It is not about risk and they have been through it and I do not have your guidance now I would be behind. How am I to deal with this without you?

He opened a book and started to read *The Life of Jesus* and wanted to learn more about Jesus.

JUDGMENT DAY

"MATTHEW DREAMT THAT THE RAPTURE TRANSCENDS
EARTH."

Matthew wants his Great Grandpa to be here because of the risk in his escapadas that he would have to do it all on his own. Had Great Grandpa been here his experience would confer an interest to Matthew who often converse with his Great Grandpa. On any adventures he is going to check, restraint or counter and seek the guidance of his Great Grandpa. Experiences these days no one teaches you, you just have to have it yourself and his Great Grandpa was a good teacher. He finds that this would be lacking for he no longer has his Great Grandpa to speak. He would have to go down to the street to find people except they were not as comforting as his Great Grandpa to speak to. How is he to find a random stranger? Thus he must do this to confer a better interest. His Great Grandpa had always compelled him to speak. Speaking was just as momentous as writing and reading. You can maneuver if you can tell other people what to do and he becomes good at it.

He had returned home to his family after Great Grandpa died where the funeral was held and along with his parents he had gained consolation from the audience who showed. They were compassionate of Great Grandpa death and most think it a natural death because Great Grandpa was nonagenarian. Though Matthew thinks Great Grandpa could have lived for another ten years because his health was thriving, but then Jesus took him away and it was time to go.

Matthew cried profusely, but no one else really shed a tear because they thought it was Great Grandpa's time to depart anyway. That he had died of old age, that his life had been long and full-filling. Matthew still thinks his Great Grand could live the next day and maybe a month or years after that. He was in dismal condition.

He is thirty five and does not have a wife. He lives a lonely life with his Great Grandpa. He had written his Great Grandpa the letters and hoped his Great Grandpa would show up again in his dream or his apparition must have been real. He still wanted the man to live for ten more years at least.

Outside, it is raining again. Great Grandpa had said that the Rapture is not going to come. Then how are they to be with each other? Great Grandpa is meant to pick a wife for him from a bunch of chic girls and now he is all by himself.

Great Grandpa you left things unsettled. You have to be here. The rapture, please implore God for the Rapture to come. I want the rapture to be here God so I can be with my Great Grandpa again. That is my only one wish.

All day Matthew stayed indoors away from the rain expecting the Rapture to come now that Jesus, who is his Great Grandpa, had ceased to live. There is no point to life anymore now that Great Grandpa is not here anymore.

Gram, how can you go without me? Dear God I pray for the Rapture to be here. I have no associates or friends. My

Great Grandpa is the only person I know. Now that you have taken him away from me, I do not know what to do and how to live my life. I do not know what to do with my time and I have no one here with me. Please hear my prayers and make the Rapture come now.

He then was lulled to sleep again and this time "he saw heaven standing open and there before him was a white horse, whose rider is called Faithful and True. With justice he judges and makes war. His eyes are like blazing fire, and on his head are many crowns. He has a name written on him that no one knows but he himself. Having the key to the bottomless pit and a great chain in his hand and the day of judgment is here with the second advent of Jesus after thousands of years."

His prayer came true and there was the Rapture.

The next morning did not happen. Where did all the humans go? The Earth was barren; there was the appearance of Armageddon. There were cracks and craters in the ground. It was the hour of dim dawn to sunrise protracted and the sun turned the color of red and cast its shadow onto the ground. Life ceased on Earth. It was back to the beginning when Earth and life had not been created and there were only vermicular/*worm in form or movement* animals that infested the dirt and Earth returned to nothing.

For days the sun kept shining its red radiance and the Earth was barren. All the people were wiped out, some went to heaven others went to hell by God's judgment. There is no one left on Earth and the people have all disappeared.

We do not care about the people who must suffer. They have malicious innards and God punished them in hell where they must endure perdition. Some go to purgatory, wash away their sins and then enter Heaven after their stages of purification. God gave them no mercy for the evil who must suffer for eternity because they are iniquitous/*evil*. He must pay for his sins on Earth.

Nothing moves in the ravaged landscape we now call Earth except the ash on the wind.

Up in Heaven Matthew had joined with his Great Grandpa in the kingdom of God. Here in heaven one never ages and remains the same. Now Matthew does not have to be without his Great Grandpa and they lived happily ever after.

He awakened and is still here. He pinched himself. He is still alive. He had only dreamt that the Rapture was really here and how the Earth would be barren. Life had not ceased on Earth. He is glad and knows that his Great Grandpa is at a good place now. Somehow he doesn't mind it and they have let him experience the Rapture for himself in a dream when all life on Earth is to end and Jesus's kingdom shall reign. He does not want that. He does not want darkness to befallen and the Rapture to end life on earth though he would be happy with his Great Grandpa.

Now he values life more. He would pray now whenever he wants to talk to his Great Grandpa but he must live and not give up the will to live. Thereby Jesus had not wanted to end life when it is a beautiful place. Though some say we are only here to suffer pain, illness, and aging. Isn't that a beautiful journey though? How life germinates.

Of course life is not compared to Heaven but I missed life or indeed this is heaven we are living in. And it goes on forever. I think there is heaven too for the afterlife. God would never end life on Earth. Maybe there is resurrection and Great Grandpa will live again for life to keep regenerating. This world is too beautiful to end.

"Live Matthew. Be educated. Read, write and speak. Learn Matthew. You are innocent and have not experienced it. You must go out there and experience it on your own. Maybe try to fall in love for the first time. Great Grandpa has nurtured you. There is a reason for God's doing. That is why he takes me away so that you would be able to grow. Live life with color and not dwell in shadow. The convention of life is going to be here long and earth is going to persist. I know you are going to be on your own. I still chose it because you will experience it on your own. Go out there and advance," a voice of his Great Grandpa said.

There was rain and thunder again and I had the window opened to let in the air through the net of the window and let it cool.

When the day that the Rapture comes there will be eternal sunlight and the Earth does not fall into darkness. It is just like the beginning when God first created the Earth when there was no life on Earth and it begins the genesis again. The Earth is no longer in use and now there is heaven or the underworld. The Earth is left dormant and the ocean and the waves billow out. Mankind has used this place now life has ceased to exist and it is to return to the original. This place would be transformed.

Matthew awakened the next day. Life is back to the original when there is life on Earth. His Great Grandpa's will was for him to live well. Death eventually comes. This place is too beautiful for all to end and it is meant for the next life to transpire.

Matthew sat there at the bench thinking. Today the rain had stopped as he had awakened. There was too much to lose even when he had nothing. Jesus would never let the end of the world take place because humans have much to live for and this venue that we have vested in is extravagant to relinquish. Life is full of colors that one should not give up life. His Great Grandpa wanted him to know this. He must shape up himself.

What must he do now? While there is nothing he knows of but the experience gained by talking to his Gram he does not know how life is going to be and how he is going to continue the generation and pass on forward. He does not know how to be a husband and how to raise a family like his Great Grandpa have passed on to him. How to be an adult in a relationship. There is no more guide and no nothing to live by. He used to have the tradition and teachings of his Great Grandpa and with aging is knowledge most of the time.

How is he to live now without the guide of his Great Grandpa the years after that. How must he live his faith? How is he to be a person and live life? If his Great Grandpa was living how would he want Matthew to live his life? What future prospects do you think he will be vested? He is in complete liberation and has no obligation.

Matthew became heartfelt as he said without his Great Grandpa for his Great Grandpa was always there and he cried.

So it happened today. That he finds out the hard way that one must let go of something that means something special then it is more difficult. Matthew does not have relations with anyone and finds it excruciating that he would ever be without his Great Grandpa. His memories lived for eternity.

Matthew remembers the story of his Great Grandpa when he was living and the story continues. Maybe they are to meet him again and the story ought to take place again. He would do it differently and always be by his side. So once upon a time it was this.

My Great Grandpa and I lived in the suburbs back at home when I was younger. He had been here with me my whole entire life as my friend, family, and teacher. If he was living he would tell me everything to do. We would fly the kite for an interim of time while he tells us his life stories about how it requires patients and he bestowed on us this gift. Coherency comes from patients and we have to hone this gift. He teaches us how to direct order in having an austere voice to command which you wanted said. My Great Grandpa is this authority. This cogent/*convincing* authority comes from him that I must replicate and still do not know today. I cannot get others to do as I pleased. They do not listen. I keep trying for people to listen to me articulate. When my Great Grandpa was there they would listen, there would be nothing without my Great Grandpa. I am glad I made it with my Great Grandpa.

The next day we were to visit the used bookstore together. We would go to the bookstore and pick a whole bucket of books together. They were on sale for $.50 to $1.00 for a book. We often get a full shelf of books and read them together. Great Grandpa had money and paid for the books. The money was from his retirement. He used to be a carpenter and built homes.

I remember a time when we flew a kite together and it was the sort of memories that you remember for life because you were with someone you loved and we talked of axioms/*principles* that were meaningful to us. I remember him telling me that in life we just have to conquer the obstacles that come across our walks of life and thrive. We keep ourselves at a constant pace like flying this kite. It requires the wind as a synergistic force and that we are helped by our ancestors. So when he is not here, he is still the synergistic force that helps the kite glide. He and his ancestors are the wind forces that drive the whole reaction, but you need to have a reaction and supplies, pick a good day and time. On days that aren't meant for kite flying the kite will never fly. We have to pick good timing and measure our progress. When good times are not here then the synergistic force will never happen. Then we are not meant for it. This is never the case but we have to choose the right circumstances and do not bombard ourselves.

Great Grandpa took the kite and let go of the kite when I pulled on it and ran with it full speed. I wanted to impress my Great Grandpa and let the kite go up high rise in the sky. I wanted it to stay up in the sky forever how I want to be with my Great Grandpa always. Then we had the kite up in the sky and I held onto the string and let my Great Grandpa hold onto it. We sat down and the kite remained in the air flying at full speed. The synergistic of the winds encompassed the kite and it was able to fly at full speed. I always remember this synergistic effect of the wind as my Great Grandpa who worked his wisdom on the other side.

I sojourned at the library today studying for my exam. One person keeps getting up and another comes to the station. People departed and ingressed all afternoon to evening. When will the time be that you meet a person like my Great Grandpa. I don't think I will ever meet another person like him. In return I want to be like him to exemplify his traits and character. Then we shall meet this incredible person again.

This writing is in tribute to my Grandpa.

Illusion of Love

"Matthew found love, is engaged, and married."

I wrote more about Matthew.

We proclaimed and glorified the gospel and herald to the songs at Church on Sunday morning. The father spoke of judgment. His wisdom conferred judgment and the proclamation of the truth is an enhanced quality. To have judgment is good. Therefore we await Judgment Day.

The air feels cool on an autumn evening after the day is finished and Matthew walks outside to his vehicle recollecting his Great Grandpa. The last encounter he has not forgotten. He recalled it all and the mysticism that is conferred. What it conferred was good to him. He recalled the memory of seeing his Great Grandpa. Something like his apparition has descended and spoken to Matthew in his dream. The dream was real and he can still remember its exact details. For several years now he has been thinking about it and how much it had meant to him that his Great Grandpa had appeared. He had appeared with Jesus and the angel Gabriel.

He had been warned of the apocalypse. He does not want it and chooses the apocalypse to not be here. He wanted life to remain because of the instances of postapocalypse that were barren. He had relieved himself from it knowing that tomorrow is still here and that the end had not yet come. He learned to savor life though he had missed living with his Great Grandpa.

There would be moments when he recalled the instances with his Great Grandpa telling him stories. He encouraged Matthew to be contemplative and act. Always think. There is clarity in purpose that is our labor and clarity requires contemplation. Therefore it is always good to be contemplative. Matthew has these musings of his Great Grandpa and remains contemplative.

On any day, he is contemplative of any action. To have clarity in purpose is what we must have. Matthew contemplates excessively and decides for his purpose in every action that is perpetrated. Today he was done with his work and again he recalled his Great Grandpa. If he was here again he would have someone to reason it out. He would have someone to listen to and someone to confide in. Now he is alone.

In the evening he might go to a fancy restaurant with Anna. They have been talking and if Great Grandpa was here he would know all about it. He had introduced to Great Grandpa the lass/*girl* before. They had lost touch for a time and one day amidst his solitary he was exhilarated to receive a call from Anna.

Somehow practicing the guitar was repetition. It lets the mind go freely and play the music that the heart aspires to hear. Matthew thinks of his Great Grandpa when playing the guitar.

I feel that I live in luxury because I have no responsibility other than the responsibility I have for myself. I did not have to take care of anybody. It was not my initiative to have to make priority for things that do not involve myself. I was being contemplative and to live with a clarity in purpose.

When my Great Grandpa was alive I had him to take care of and now all the responsibility is uplifted. Since I got used to it, not being there is a burden. I used to have the responsibility of pushing my Great Grandpa and taking walks with him in the evening. I enjoyed much of it. The evening hour reminds me of the time when we would go out on our evening jaunts.

Hence there was a lot of time and a lot of free time. Nowadays there is nothing to do without a companion. He had to seek companionship. When Anna called he was playing his guitar and finding solitude pleasure in music. He was glad to hear from her. He updated her on the news of which had surpassed and the passing away of his Great Grandpa in which they had the funeral. He did not have the time to inform her of it.

"I am so sorry for your hurt. If there is anything I can do to make you feel better. He was such an intellectual man. I really enjoyed his company the last time we went out. He told me the story of the defenseless. I was thankful for his lessons. That we need to defend the defenseless. From that time on I always stand up for myself if I can and seek help whenever I am defenseless, though I try not to be," said Anna.

"Great Grandpa knows plethora didn't mind giving you a hand because he thinks you might be here for me. Not sure if he was talking about you being defenseless or myself. Don't think it is yourself who is defenseless. I think he means me. I am not as smart or outgoing as you. I can never do anything on my feet. If I learn to think more then my mind would not be blank when the situation calls for it. In other words, he means I am defenseless and for you to be my friend," said Matthew.

"It is a great loss that he is no longer living. Are you okay now Matthew, I know you are by yourself here and have no one other than yourself. Of course I am your friend," said Anna.

"It must be alright now. I was just seeking a companion when you called. It's great Anna. The world is like that, no one concerns the business of another person and you live your life knowing your own business. I missed my Great Grandpa," said Matthew.

"I understand. If there is any way I can help I am here if you need or want anything. Just listen to your Great Grandpa and be happy. There is nothing but to live a happy life come to realize it. Time will heal everything so don't burden yourself with any trouble. I want to take you to church. Let's go next time we'll pray for your Great Grandpa together. I want to especially gratify and give tribute to him for helping me, to be a good person," said Anna.

Next Sunday they attended Holy Spirits where we prayed for Matthew's Great Grandpa. Matthew and Anna kneeled at the pew to dedicate a prayer to his Grandpa. Matthew knew his Great Grandpa was listening to his prayer and was there in presence with

God. He would be prepared when Jesus comes again. The last time he did not want the apocalypse to be here and asked Jesus to make life continue on this earth. He was not prepared to go and leave the world to be a barren place. Now he must prepare himself, he has too much time on his hands without responsibilities for anything that he wondered about his vocation on this earth. What is he set out to do and what does he need to accomplish? He needed to have purpose and accomplishments. His Great Grandpa had done plenty in his lifetime including the aspect of raising Matthew. He would raise children. Perhaps that is what he needed to do.

Great Grandpa had been happy with Anna when I and her had been going out. Maybe he would ask her to marry him and raise a family with him. Anna was kneeling next to him on the pew and he was thinking it to himself and to his Great Grandpa.

"I hope you are doing well in heaven. I know that is where you have gone and may your life in heaven be well," said Matthew.

"We will come and pray for you every week and I hope you shine light on Matthew as he approaches the road on his own and not have anybody to confide in. Please be with him always," said Anna.

We rest for a moment in silence to think of Matthew's Great Grandpa. They were the only two left after the church was dismissed. Father Timothy was still around if we had any concerns and Matthew asked Father Timothy to pray for his Great Grandpa. He had promised to pray for his Great Grandpa. He could be contacted anytime to speak with and Matthew plans on coming to speak to him about the Rapture and what he thinks should take place if Jesus were to give him a choice whether the Rapture should be here. Matthew had chosen for life to persist though he had wanted to be with his Great Grandpa in heaven, but somehow he didn't want life to end on earth because it was a beautiful creation. This Earth would be barren without life in the apocalypse. Matthew did not want that although he knew one day he would die. He knows what happens after that his soul shall be judged and he shall await judgment day. He still did not want Earth to cease in existence. Maybe there is a second life when everyone would get to live again. Where would he go after he dies? He would return to ashes, he had been taught this. Would his soul still live on? Would he still be conscious? Is there an entity that exists that was remnant of him? What would he accomplished? Matthew thought of the time that he has, he still has too much time and does not know what to do with it. He has to expand his circle and find someone to talk to. Father Timothy was ideal. He knows much of religion and Matthew was interested in it.

Matthew did not have a vocation, but no way was ready to die. Although he did want it to be the end of the world so that he could be with his Great Grandpa when he discovered that the Earth would be barren he did not fancify the idea positively.

"Well, when your time is ready you will be prepared to go, you are still young and haven't lived long enough to want to further your life for eternity. You have to expect Jesus when he comes," said Father Timothy.

Matthew wants to ask Father Timothy why the Earth becomes a barren and desolate place after we die and the apocalypse comes like in the dream that he had but he was not sure his visions are the same as the apocalypse. Maybe it was personal to him to see such barrenness and he did not want to divulge it to anybody. He had seen the image in his dream. What if the Father shared the same vision? It was worth a try but he needed to do more research on it. Why can't Jesus leave the Earth to be a vivacious place like the Garden of Eden when the end is here? Why does life have to cease? After all it is a conjecture of what might occur in the rapture and not really factual so he does not want to disturb the father. But the image is somewhere in a book.

In any case, when he was ready he would seek help from Father Timothy who seemed amiable but at the same time intimidating. We go to Holy Spirits every week to catch Father Timothy's sermon and learn something insightful or knowledgeable. Father Timothy and Matthew have never spoken although he was the father at confession and he hears his sermon some weekends. Matthew is introverted and kept to himself although he wishes to speak to the father. He would have to prepare himself and do research. When Great Grandpa was alive he would have someone to speak to and they would attend Church together. Now he was going with Anna who was good to have around.

"Where are we going now after this?" asked Anna.

"I do not know. I have nowhere to go but back to my apartment. I am good with you as a conversant. We can keep talking that way I would not be solitary without my Great Grandpa," said Matthew.

"Do you want to go out? Maybe we should go watch the stars. There are shooting stars tonight. We should stargaze. I am here and you do not need to be alone," said Anna.

I was glad Anna was there for me. We would go to dinner and after I would play the guitar to serenade her for this occasion that we are first going out. We thought of getting married.

Great Grandpa would be proud of me if he noticed the wedding will be here. This instant is exhilarating and I want to share it with him the most.

I delight in this moment of sharing and joy. That I unravel piecemeal to my audience of the incident. Judgment day will come or not I do not know, I enjoy life to the fullest is what my Great Grandpa had entrusted and endowed to me. I would love for one day to be with my Great Grandpa whenever judgment day would be. This moment is serenity, peace, and joy. As I share this with the audience.

Anna was beautiful that day. I remembered to tell you this Great Grandpa that I met a beautiful girl and she became my bride. We all hope well and a happy ending in the end. We had a celebration and it was a festival. You could have been there or where are you now, do you speculate? I believe people go to heaven and they watch down from above to see the actions that happen to mankind. I believe that you are still living. There isn't a happier day than the day of our wedding but it could have been better with you being here most definitely. I keep thinking about it, Great Grandpa that if you are living or I know somewhere you are still in existence. There would be the best for us and we would get your blessing when we marry off. Anyway, I wished you were here and there isn't a moment that I live without thinking of you and being with profundity of thought so that my brain would work better. I will always remember what you have done for me and the sacrifices that you made to raise me when I was growing up and I hope I wasn't much trouble. Anna wanted me to make a speech and I wrote up one and then delivered it to our large audience at the ceremony. I didn't have many friends and was esoteric/*recondite* but Anna had rapport/*friends* from every corner so all her friends were invited to the party. The garden was filled in the morning and at night the hall was filled with guests.

It was a happy day for me and I just want to share it with you, Great Grandpa. I felt special that I was invited to make a speech and I thought of you. I first wanted to commemorate everyone for coming to the wedding and to solve this mystery it is Anna and Matthew.

There are heartfelt moments in life you just have to remember as I am standing here delivering a speech to the audience. I feel much gratitude and am grateful that you all show.

I am just a stranger, standing up here making a speech and you might remember someday at our wedding that I have said this to you that you should cherish the person next to you because when you look around you they are there and when they are not there anymore...it is a loss. But we don't want to talk about that today.

Today is a happy day and we talk of the good things that are happening and they are all here to celebrate with us on this day, the festival of our wedding. I say hold on to the one you love and you can hold on to them even when they are mad at you and do not want it because they have to be away and it means the world to you that they are here. Don't ever let them go and you will get what you want. Even if they are gone, out there busy somewhere and can't be here they are with us here in spirit. There is never anyone who I know who would miss this moment. I speak of Anna, that she means the world to me, when no one was there she came into my life and cheered me up so let's cheer for Anna and Matthew today.

I was thinking of my Great Grandpa partially when I thought of what to write. I always think of my Great Grandpa when I needed inspiration. Thoughts of him are expounding and I can extract the idea from his personages and sometimes try to impersonate him. He is a dignitary figure and I respect him very much. Anna I felt the same, that is why she is my wife. Throughout the years we lived together I learned more about her and she learned about me. Just like we used to Great Grandpa.

There was no trouble except I had too much time. I wasn't doing much. I still like it better when Great Grandpa was here. Anna is different and cannot supersede Great Grandpa. Anyway I planned our wedding. Enough of Anna for now.

Besides that I had nothing planned. The day begins the same every day and I discovered that I have too much time. I have no one to follow around any longer and have to find things to do when I have no passion in anything except to play the guitar and speak. Maybe I can become a speech writer and give inspirational speeches. I like delivering speeches as much as writing them. I have been practicing my writing and perhaps developed a career doing that.

Reading. I spent most of my time reading. I don't know what I would do without your companion because there isn't anybody who cares. You and I had each other but now you had to be gone and I have no one. I am glad of Anna, but sometimes she doesn't exist because I made her up because there isn't anybody as near perfect out there that I would marry compared to Anna, the one you had met, but then she was nowhere to be found. People do not want me. So for the duration of the time being I had much time on hand and didn't know what to do with it. I had a lot of time. I spent it speaking, reading, writing, sleeping and eating all on my own. I didn't have time sometimes when I got involved but when I wasn't imbibed in it there was much leisure time. I did nothing with time, but I'm still glad that time is ad libitum.

THE BEGINNING AND THE ENDING

"MATTHEW AND ANNA GREW OLD AND LIVED HAPPILY
EVER AFTER."

It is autumn. One more year has taken place and he is listening to the first rain of the year. The seasons kept passing by and he kept himself the same. Time is swift yet he still does not have a means to get by it without falling behind and not doing anything. Though he is glad it is autumn and he is going to jaunt out again to see the changes of nature. It begins to rain heavily now and Matthew watches out the window. It reminds him of ancient days with his Great Grandpa whenever he smelled the cement after the rain. He must get over it now even though he has fruition it will never happen. He would always desire his Great Grandpa to be present. He can never cease thinking of it even though it is already the next season.

The next season is here and he prepares himself to welcome autumn. Changes take place to his surroundings although Matthew manages to stay the same. He had not noticed any differences after the years had passed and every day there were incidences. He would jaunt the street to obtain some verve and come back to his apartment and write of it. Nature is beautiful once Autumn is here and the scenery evolves leaving estival/*summer* behind. There are still some remnants of estival though the leaves are turning its color from emerald to orange, red, and brown.

The rain is not insipid/*boring*. He does not get bored watching the rain fall. It lulls him to sleep on a day when there is nonevent. He thinks of solitude and thinks about how he is going to get himself a visitor to come by and converse with him. He has no visitors. Somehow, someone is going to enter his path and speak to him and how he would be like anybody else. He would have a social life.

He reads and wonders about the account that he reads. He wishes someone was here and changed things for him so that he would not be in this monotonous situation any longer. That he would be able to reach out to someone. He knows that was not possible. No miracle is going to happen for him to be involved. He had better search for himself. Maybe he should look for work. But he had work, that is emceeing or writing.

On New Year's Day he spent time watching the snow outside the window. It is tranquil and he reflects on the year. He is happy on his own, but he misses his Great Grandpa. His New Year's resolution was to meet more people and expand his social circle. He doesn't know if that was possible to reach out because he doesn't know anyone. It was the last day of the old year. He doesn't know if today will be it, that the Rapture is going to be here. He wants to consume himself in the dream again. He still remembers that one time when Jesus, his Great Grandpa and the angel appeared. Would it be time now? He has enjoyed this Earth. Though he doesn't have a purpose. He was lacking a purpose. Father Timothy had said to do everything with clarity in purpose. For the time being he was happy. Maybe that was his purpose. He does everything to keep himself happy whenever he can accommodate. Though least was required of him and he tried to cultivate. It was in his personality that was formulated maybe if he had been inculcated. Matthew had an extravagant personality. It was not in one's personality, but one's capability of bringing happiness. In the end he had persuaded himself that it was to be happy. His purpose is to be happy. That should be it. He remembers three factors that kept him happy. He should have something he loves to do, someone to love and something to look forward to. That is the means to happiness. Whenever it is, he would refer to these means of happiness. He has a goal. His goal is to perfect his writing and enhance it.

Matthew continues to read, write, and speak his normal routine. Maybe then he would be around people. There were going to be changes and hopefully all his dreams would come true.

Tonight, the last of the year, the snow continues to fall. He kept his window open to hear the sounds of the snowfall and get a chill in his warm room while he had the furnace turned on. It was a good feeling. All night he could not fall asleep. He was thinking how fortunate his life is and that he didn't need anything else.

He didn't have an obligation or was forced to do anything. School was over for him and his work he liked very much to produce writing. Though he is never done learning. He had no complaints to make and was ready to come home in a few days. He thought of coming home and fell asleep.

In several days, he returned to his apartment and flew home. He came home with Anna. His parents were proud of him.

Love at this point means the world to him. He was overwhelmed with filial and carnal love. Certainly, he had someone to love and this made his purpose happy. He couldn't explain how overjoyed he was and certainly there were the people he loved. They picked him up at the airport and he felt himself a grown person. It was crowded with love and joy. His life couldn't be better and knew he had time for one more day. No, he did not just have one more day but he had the rest of his life to be here with his parents. There is one moment of joy and one moment of pain. It intertwines and one departs, exists and another emotion ingresses. We slowly enter springtime again and leave the bleak winter behind. One door closes and another door opens. It is the end of one and the beginning of another. This is just the beginning.

Matthew likes the beginning because it is the emblem of happiness. He doesn't like things ending compared to the beginning though all things must have a way of resolution.

Anna was by my side when I came home. We would have a life here. We live happily ever after, except on some occasions we fought but it was never to mention it. It springs out of love and when two people have to get along it is such. We fought over little things and we laughed over it because we think of how much we love each other. I was ready for the new relationships that involved Anna. Most of the time we are happy and I maintained my purpose. Anna was always there for me and we talked all the time.

Over dinner one evening, Matthew and Anna were talking of their daily life occurrences and expectations.

"Now that we're married you need to come to your attention that you aren't alone anymore and have responsibilities as my husband," said Anna.

Matthew was not alone anymore with the companion of Anna and he was not living like he was before in recluse. Marriage life mustered up much entertainment for him as he was with a companion and didn't have to be by himself out in the world. Now he had moved back with his parents so the conditions were different and he had someone there with him all the time. Anna's existence was a treasure to Matthew who knew no one. Just her presence lightened him up and by God's coincidence they had met again one day. He can never have enough of Anna and thoughts of her were sanguine and optimistic. He gets cheerful, hopeful, and aplomb/*self-assurance* being around Anna.

"Where have you been all this time? Never mention to me these times where you have been off to? I didn't know to expect you when you came into my life," said Matthew.

"I have been working to become an attorney. I am pursuing a career in law. I am busy most of the time," said Anna.

Anna was sent to him from Heaven. She was outgoing, extroverted, and smart; he can never compare himself to Anna.

"I finally called you because you impressed me. You are very well articulated," said Anna.

Matthew didn't know that Anna was impressed at his articulation and loved her for it. Anna was an attorney and her articulation is just as pronounced as Matthew. They would act out in court at times to help Anna and Anna would be the lawyer and he would give testimony. It is difficult to maneuver but he manages to do it with the gifts that his Great Grandpa bestowed on him.

All couples have tribulations and they resolve in the end, one time Anna and Matthew got into a fight when he messed up her practice. They were practicing court and Matthew was uncooperative. He infuriated Anna. Anna insisted on deleting their files together and Matthew did not stop her and she deleted the files and had to do the work all over again. She remains sullen at him for days.

"There is no use in replacing the files because I already deleted them. I would never practice with you again," said Anna.

"Why did you have to delete the files?"

"Because you didn't stop me and you suggested! You ignoramus! Why did you suggest it? I went along to think that you didn't like me having it so I deleted it because you were part of the inspiration! Now I never need you to practice any more and can do it on my own," said Anna.

"You shouldn't use it, my ideas aren't great anyway," said Matthew.

"But it's a waste of time coming up with new scripts. What if I were to delete your writing? You would hate me for it," said Anna.

Part of the fantod/*unreasonable* would not resolve until there is eventuation Matthew learned. Until Anna was with Matthew she would still be angry with him and they would still have problems. One cannot yield. The scale would be imbalanced. They have to work it out 50/50 and 50% there is a feast.

Matthew spent a week after that trying to replicate the files and return it to Anna. With his innovation Anna was no longer upset with Matthew and was impressed.

"These are my new ideas; they are all splendid compared to what was scribbled," said Matthew.

Anna quit being mad at Matthew after that and they made up by going to the restaurant. Their lives were in tranquility and some matters might upset them and they would resolve it. It was Matthew's way of getting attention from Anna because Anna was always busy with school work. All Matthew could do was help her and he helped her most of the time and there were times when Matthew was not perfect he would be yelled at by Anna. Anna being stressed out would yell at Matthew over the most inane of situations. He would yell back and they would not talk to each other for days. Life is a turmoil for the couple who were contending to make a living and there was frolic and play making up many memories that they shared.

Whenever Anna takes off, Matthew would get teary. He missed a companion. He was not sure if this was real. What he had built with Anna. Sometimes Anna goes off somewhere for her business trip and Matthew remains at home he would worry and miss her much. He was attached to Anna just like his Great Grandpa. It was not a replacement, but with company Matthew feels much better. How can anybody be replaced? Matthew realized everybody has a role in his life and if they were gone he would miss them very much. He cherished the relationship that he has with his mom and dad. He hasn't thought of it yet but one day his parents are going to grow old and they did. They lived their lives well and gave lessons to Matthew. They spent the rest of their days traveling across the world.

"I want to live until I am old with you," said Matthew. "I want to be like my Great Grandpa, he lived a full-filled life."

"Of course I am there for you, you're my husband," said Anna to Matthew.

Together they joined hands in songs and cherished the moments they have with each other. The years they lived together there were moments when Anna and

Matthew fought and didn't get along. They make up and make peace with each other and resolve issues. They grew in number and Anna and Matthew had many children and grandchildren together.

Throughout the years that they lived Matthew never forgot his Great Grandpa and conjured him up on occasion and told the stories to his children and grandchildren.

"Your great grandpa was a magnificent man, he lived a legacy and passed it on to me his will to become the amazing person that I am," said Matthew.

He tries to impersonate his Great Grandpa while raising his children. He tells them stories like he used to be told that contain the lessons of life that are unforgettable, just like his Great Grandpa is unforgettable. Matthew learns to have duties and responsibilities toward his children and he grows up. When his duty is done then he can rest. Now it was the time of the test.

Matthew did not know how to be a good parent and he went to a parenting class that set him as a role model. An adult is someone with much wisdom to talk about anything, can tell stories, is a magician to solve problems and has money to buy items. He subsidized/*supported financially* the spending on his children and gave them everything.

Primarily, he taught his kids how to articulate, how to read and how to write. Articulation/*eloquence in speaking* was a gift that his Great Grandpa bestowed to him. He always remembers to have eloquence when he can and bestowed that to his children. Primarily, they never taught it in school to articulate, you have to gain it on your own. Matthew was there readily so that his children had someone to talk to. The children he raised become smart, astute, and competent.

In the end, Matthew grows along with Anna and one morning they sit themselves on the bench at the park thinking back to the moments when they were young. Life has been a journey.

"I told you life is a journey and not just a destination. You have lived a happy life haven't you? There is nothing to worry about growing old," said Anna.

"I don't worry Anna, if it doesn't bother you being married to someone as old fashioned and traditional as I am. I know you're very up to date. I think of a new perspective now," said Matthew.

"Does it still come to you? Jesus' vision?"

"I remember it, it has been so long ago when I was a young lad that Jesus visited me in my dream," said Matthew.

"You talk of it all the time, and it reminds you of your Great Grandpa. Everytime you talk of your Great Grandpa you remind me of the Rapture," said Anna.

"It has been years and still no signs of it. This earth is going to keep regenerating itself and keep living on for one generation to continue the next," said Matthew.

"Do you think the Rapture is going to be here now that we are nonagenarian? We would be your Great Grandpa age when he passed away," said Anna.

"I would never want it to be the Rapture because the earth would be barren. There are no differences now. Death awaits when I need to go then it is time to go. That is that. Like my Great Grandpa when he had to depart from us, it just happens."

"What about those young dreams of yours? I remember you used to be insane over the Rapture and you hoped it would come so you would be with your Great Grandpa. Those days you told me about it," said Anna.

"Isn't the earth a lovely place? We finish using it and then another generation is going to be born and use the same space that we operated to make a living. I never want the end of the world to come for my children and grandchildren to have life on this earth," said Matthew.

"I am glad you think it now? But isn't there something you haven't figured out about the Rapture? Why Jesus's apparition appears to you?" asked Anna.

"I think my Great Grandpa is Jesus and he just wants me to live a happy life and I did live a happy life. I am still living it now as a nonagenarian. I don't know when it is time to go, but I would be my Great

Grandpa's age now he has to be 150 years old or older in heaven if that is what is. When it is time to go then I am ready. I guess I didn't have to mob over his death because part of living is realizing that death would come. I have enough time already and would not mind when Jesus calls me to go," said Matthew.

"As long as I am with you I am not afraid Matthew Benjamin Pham," said Anna.

"I missed you too if I was gone from this earth. You helped me raise my children and grandchildren. You did a lovely job in life when Jesus calls you or me away we'll wait on each other. If you go first then I will follow you. You do the same, if I go first you will be here then just follow me. Just follow me Anna," said Matthew.

"I want to go before you, that way I will not be here alone by myself. I can't take loneliness. I think if you go I will make sure to follow you," said Anna.

"Then make sure to yourself, Anna," said Matthew.

The couple hold hands while Anna walks with a gurney and Matthew walks with a cane. They walked their steps and Anna followed Matthew to the end of this earth.

When he passed away he went to heaven and lived with his Great Grandpa. Matthew, an upright and sanguine man who enhanced the words of his Great Grandpa, has lived a life of plenty. In conclusion, I think life is lived and lived to the fullest. There was particular interest in the measure of one's life. That one has three things; family, a house, and career. Life has been pleasant and mild for a lonely citizen.

Anna follows Matthew to heaven and appends their lineages giving him many children. The children are an obstacle, but they are loved and cared for. Anna is feisty, loving and a person of authority. She is raised in an educated environment that is due to her much sophistry and became an attorney. Anna is an aggressive woman, outspoken wife, tender mother and erudite grandmother.

I say the children are an obstacle because I grew up with seven siblings, myself included. Such a long journey it has been an evening of an author in creating the character named Matthew. Whose is filial because it is my nephew that my Grandpa had sent me in a dream to pen about him and the Rapture. He is the first of the new generation that we hope to cultivate this century. All this is about the words of Grandpa Phu and there is our ancestral tree. We want to ingrain the new generation to remember our ancestors. It has been a joy!

SPECIAL ADDITION

A LETTER FROM THE FOUNDER

Somehow mystical, she is a faithful one-time student in chastity and built by the faculties/*powers* vested from her Grandpa many generations ago. The strongest power of all that she inherits is chastity and she learned this grace to preserve that saved her whole family at minor sacrifices, being patina.

There are in the end three things that last: faith, hope and love and the greatest of these is Love. But the happiest in my opinion, is *Hope*. So then she lives every day of her cherished life in happiness with her filial family singly passed the coming of age.

This book is made possible by her Grandpa and the founder lived to pass on what her Grandpa bequeathed to the scions of the next generation and many more days to come. We always remember what our ancestors sacrificed/say to make us enabled in this foreign nation. They lived with no guilt as we promised.